TRUE TALES OF
OLD ALEXANDRIA

TRUE TALES OF
OLD ALEXANDRIA

TED PULLIAM

THE
History
PRESS

Published by The History Press
Charleston, SC
www.historypress.com

Back cover: The Alexandria waterfront, 1895. *Patrick O'Brien*.

First published 2023

Manufactured in the United States

ISBN 9781467154765

Library of Congress Control Number: 2023937210

To Molly

CONTENTS

ACKNOWLEDGEMENTS

I am grateful for the extremely capable assistance provided me in the preparation of this book by the following:

The staff of the Alexandria Library Special Collections/Local History branch from the time it was located in the Lloyd House to the present, particularly George Combs.

The people at Alexandria Archaeology, particularly Pam Cressey, Fran Bromberg, Eleanor Breen, Ben Skolnik, Ruth Reeder, Emma Richardson, Elizabeth Field and Jennifer Barker.

The staffs at various publications who previously printed articles that became chapters in this book, including Steve Maurin, John Kelly, Brooks Stoddard, Linda Greenberg and Joel Chineson.

The readers of various chapters for their comments and encouragement: Jim Johnston, Maya Fitzgerald, Andrew McElwain and Lee Ness.

The Café du Soleil coffee guys, Jay Roberts and Dave Cavanaugh, for their enthusiastic support.

Rita Holtz for her wonderful help with images.

Kate Jenkins, Zoe Ames and the rest of the staff at The History Press.

My wife, Molly, for her patience and marvelous support in many ways.

MOST OF THESE CHAPTERS are composed of articles written several years ago. Many people helped with their research, composition and publication, but because of the passage of time, I am afraid I may have missed acknowledging some whose assistance was important. I apologize, but please know that your help was valuable and is appreciated.

INTRODUCTION

This book consists of eleven chapters that tell real stories of events that took place in Alexandria or the surrounding area. The stories begin at Jamestown in 1609 and on the shore across the Potomac River from the future site of Alexandria in 1623, and they end on a waterfront block under development in Old Town in 2018.

In between appear colonists, cannibals, Indians, an inept British general and a notorious seventeenth-century woman. George Washington dodges musket balls, and we meet a frightened young Union soldier, Revolutionary War gunrunners, nineteenth-century duelists and a jailed free Black girl. General George S. Patton makes an appearance, as do a mid-twentieth-century drunkard fleeing the Law, six 1920s bank robbers and other assorted personalities—all with a connection to Alexandria or nearby locations.

Eight of the chapters were published previously: *Alexandria Chronicle* published chapters 7 and 10; *Alexandria Gazette*, chapter 5; *American History* magazine, chapter 4; *Legal Times*, chapter 6; *WWII History* magazine, chapter 9; and the *Washington Post*, chapters 1 and 11. Two others were unpublished but were adapted from talks given several years ago, and one other was completed just recently.

I hope you enjoy reading them and maybe learn things unknown before about Alexandria and the area. The chapters are arranged chronologically, but of course, you may read them in any order you like. So, please begin.

Chapter 1

TRADED TO THE INDIANS

The Strange Tale of a Colonial Boy

We do not know what Henry Spelman did to deserve his punishment. What we do know is it was bad enough that his family put him on a ship and sent him halfway across the world. That's how, almost four hundred years ago, fourteen-year-old Henry ended up at Jamestown, the English colony on the banks of Virginia's James River. While nearly everyone has heard the story of Captain John Smith and Pocahontas, Henry's remarkable tale may surprise you.

When Henry arrived in 1609, the colony was struggling to survive. For two years, the colonists had very little to eat. To help with this problem, John Smith decided to trade Henry to the Indians so the boy could learn their language. If things went well, Henry would return to the colony as an interpreter. If they didn't, well, Henry was on his own.

Henry joined two other boys, Thomas Savage and a German named Samuel, who already lived with the Indians. A few weeks later, Powhatan, the leader of the Powhatan tribe, sent Henry back to Jamestown with a message: Powhatan would give the hungry English corn in exchange for copper. What Henry did not know was that it was a trap—when thirty colonists arrived to trade, Indians came out of their hiding places in the cornfields, war hatchets in hand. Only two Englishmen made it back to Jamestown alive.

During the fight, a Powhatan warrior drew his hatchet and, as Henry wrote later, "with a single stroke" killed Samuel. Henry bolted up a trail and continued moving north until finally reaching the safety of a Patawomeck village on the banks of the Potomac River.

Henry Spelman.
Steve McCracken.

Henry stayed peacefully with the Patawomecks for more than a year until he was bought for some copper pieces by an English trader who took him back across the sea to London.

But Henry had one last adventure with the Indians. He returned to Jamestown as an interpreter, and in 1623, at the age of twenty-eight, he led a trading expedition far up the Potomac River, probably near its juncture with the Anacostia River. Leaving some of his men on the boat, he went ashore with others to a village of the Nacotchtanck tribe on the Maryland side of the Potomac. Soon there was a great noise from the village. The colonists who had remained on the boat then saw "a man's head thrown down the bank" and watched it roll to the water's edge. They could not tell whose head it was, only that it was a White man's.

Henry Spelman was never seen by the English again.

HENRY'S TIME

The winter Henry spent with Powhatan was known in Jamestown as "the starving time." Before the winter, the Jamestown population was more than five hundred; after, it was no more than fifty.

During "the starving time," a colonist named Collins killed his wife, salted her down, and ate her. John Smith wrote, "Whether she was better roasted, boiled, or carbonado'd [grilled], I know not, but of such a dish as salted wife I never heard of."

Henry wrote that the Patawomeck women and children played a game that was like soccer. The men, on the other hand, would "play with a little

Algonquian village, 1590. *State Library of North Carolina.*

ball, letting it fall out of their hand, and striketh it with the top of his foot. And he that can strike the ball furthes wins what they play for."

Henry was the first non-Indian to live on the Potomac River. His village, Passapatanzy, probably was located about ten miles east of present-day Fredericksburg.

In 1613, at age eighteen, Henry wrote about his experiences with the Indians. The manuscript was not found until the 1800s and printed in 1872.

Chapter 2

THE NOTORIOUS
MARGARET BRENT

The first European who owned land in what would become Alexandria was the remarkable Englishwoman Margaret Brent, and she received that first land grant over 350 years ago.

Margaret first came from England to Maryland—not Virginia. She came there in 1638 with her sister Mary and her brothers, Giles and Fulke. Margaret was thirty-seven years old and unmarried when she arrived in Maryland, and she remained unmarried throughout her life, although in Maryland at that time, men outnumbered women six to one. She came from a strong Catholic family (two sisters who remained in England became nuns), and one historian speculated that Margaret remained unmarried because, although she did not become a nun, she took a vow of celibacy for religious reasons.

Regardless of her reasons, it probably was good that she did not marry. In Maryland then, married women had limited control over property, but unmarried women were legally allowed to own property and manage it themselves.

Margaret and her sister soon became landowners and established a home independent of their brothers. Margaret managed her land and business as a man would have done then and appeared frequently in court to collect debts, winning more cases than she lost. Her court appearances were unusual for a woman at that time. In fact, she appeared in court so often that Maryland court records sometimes referred to her as "Margaret Brent, Gent. [Gentleman]."

The Brents were distant cousins of the governor of Maryland, Leonard Calvert, and his brother the proprietor (owner) of Maryland, Lord Baltimore. Margaret had a particularly close relationship with Governor Calvert. He respected Margaret's business judgement so much that when he died in June 1647, he named her as the sole executor of his estate.

Margaret proved to be a capable executor, so much so that six months later, the Maryland Provincial Court also appointed her as the local attorney for the proprietor himself, Lord Baltimore, who remained in England.

Soon after being appointed Lord Baltimore's representative, Margaret made a remarkable request to the Maryland legislature. She asked that she be allowed two votes in the legislative assembly, one in her own right and one as the attorney for Lord Baltimore. No woman had even one vote in the assembly then, and despite her position and her competence, the all-male legislature promptly turned down the request, denying her any vote whatsoever.

That may have been an omen, for the next year, things began to go badly for the Brents in Maryland. In fact, Margaret's brother Giles thought it wise to leave Maryland and cross the Potomac River to settle in Virginia because he had angered the powerful Lord Baltimore.

Margaret Brent seeks votes from the Maryland Assembly. *National Park Service/Louis Glanzman.*

The most prominent cause of Lord Baltimore's anger with Giles was that, a few years earlier, Giles had married an eleven-year-old orphaned Indian princess. The girl had been raised by Margaret Brent and Catholic missionaries after the death of her father, who had been the tayac, or "king," of the Piscataway Indians. Apparently, Giles hoped that through this marriage to the daughter of an Indian king, he would acquire a claim to much of Maryland. Lord Baltimore himself, however, claimed all of Maryland through a grant from King Charles I, and he was not pleased.

As a result, in 1648, Giles left Maryland for Virginia accompanied by his young Indian wife. They settled at Aquia Creek, about thirty-five miles south of the future Alexandria, making Giles then the northernmost European on the Virginia side of the Potomac.

Shortly afterward, Margaret also had some disagreements with Lord Baltimore and joined her brother in Virginia.

However, the Brents prospered in this new location, in part because their move to Virginia came shortly before a land rush for property along the Potomac River. Earlier, a Virginia treaty with the Powhatan Indians had prevented colonists from settling north of the York River, but in 1649, Virginia unilaterally nullified it. During the following thirty years, land grants were made for thousands of acres along the Potomac waterfront.

As part of this rush for land, in 1654, when Margaret was in her early fifties, she sought and received a grant for seven hundred acres on Great Hunting Creek (the southern border of present-day Alexandria). This land included much of present-day Old Town.

Margaret probably had never seen the property before she bought it. There were no roads in that part of northern Virginia then, and the area's only inhabitants were Indians, whose friendship with Europeans was questionable.

What Margaret did with the property is unclear, but Virginia law at that time required "seating and planting" the property within three years, or someone else could claim it. Later, the Virginia Assembly defined "seating and planting": "Building an house and keeping a stock one whole year upon the land shall be accounted seating; and that cleering, tending and planting an acre of ground shall be accounted planting." One observer later reported that many patentees "cut down a few trees and make thereof a hut covering it with bark, and turn two or three hogs into the woods by it." They then "put a little Indian corn into the ground" among the trees lying there "but take no care of their crop, nor make any further use of the land."

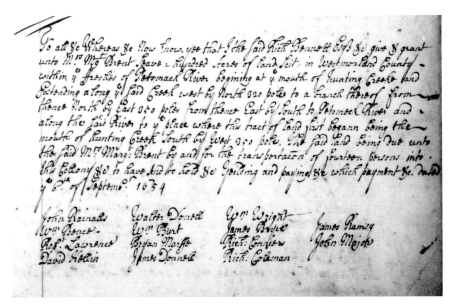

Land grant to Margaret Brent of seven hundred acres, later a part of Alexandria. *Library of Virginia.*

Although the requirement was erratically enforced, Margaret likely met it in some way, because she held onto the property. Toward the end of her life, however, she seems to have neglected it.

Then, in 1669, when Margaret was sixty-eight years old, John Alexander, a Stafford County landowner, became the owner of six thousand acres along the Potomac River that included the future sites of Arlington National Cemetery, the Pentagon, Reagan Washington National Airport and Alexandria. It also included Margaret Brent's seven hundred acres.

But for a while, no one noticed.

Then Margaret died at the age of seventy. A few years later, her heirs discovered John Alexander's purchase. They had inherited Margaret's disputatious disposition as well as the land, and they forced the Alexander heirs to purchase the property again. Moreover, while John Alexander had originally paid only one pound of tobacco an acre for the property, his heirs had to pay the Brent heirs fifteen pounds an acre.

The businesswoman in Margaret Brent would have approved.

Chapter 3

JOHN CARLYLE, WILLIAM FAIRFAX AND THE INDIANS

The Winchester Conference of 1753

I t was a little before six o'clock on a clear Monday evening in September 1753. A small group of Virginia gentlemen had gathered on a dirt road at the north end of Winchester, Virginia, a new town about sixty-five miles northwest of Alexandria. There they waited for the arrival of an important delegation from the Ohio Country, that vast area west of the Allegheny River that today is the very western part of Pennsylvania and the entire state of Ohio. Lining the road a few steps behind these gentlemen stood fifty Virginia militiamen, their muskets grounded at their sides.

This September was a year and a half before the arrival of General Edward Braddock and his British army at Alexandria at the very beginning of the French and Indian War. It also was more than twenty years before the beginning of the American Revolution.

The Virginians were led by the distinguished Colonel William Fairfax, who had been appointed by Virginia's lieutenant governor Robert Dinwiddie (who was, in effect, the royal governor of the Colony of Virginia) as his representative to this sensitive meeting with the Ohio delegation. He was joined by Thomas, the sixth Lord Fairfax (Colonel Fairfax's cousin) and Alexandrian John Carlyle, then a justice of the peace of Fairfax County (also Colonel Fairfax's son-in-law).

Soon, down the road, the Virginians saw walking toward them the delegation they were to meet—some ninety-eight Indians: men, women and children; Iroquois, Delawares, Shawnees, Wyandottes and Miamis. The

John Carlyle. *Carlyle House Historic Park/Jeff Hancock.*

warriors among them carried muskets resting on their shoulders. As soon as they sighted the Virginians, they raised their muskets, pointed them in the air and fired a salute. An observer described it as "a sheet of fire." The Virginia militiamen answered with their own volley of muskets.

With that, the diplomatic rituals had begun for the meeting between the Virginians and the Ohio Indians that would subsequently be known as the Winchester Conference. The basic source for information about the conference is the minutes recorded by a Virginian during its proceedings. The minutes still exist and can be found in the Library of Congress. They portray an unusually clear picture of the diplomacy practiced by Indians and colonists in response to the increasing tensions between the two of them, and between each of them and the French in Canada, just before the French and Indian War began.

The Conference came at a time when the relationship among the three powers with interests in the Ohio Country—the French in Canada, the British in the Atlantic seaboard colonies and the Indians, who actually lived and hunted in the Ohio Country—was changing. Each of the powers claimed that its people alone owned these lands. But recently, the French had begun taking new, more aggressive actions to assert their claim.

These French actions were viewed by both the British colonists and the Indians with increasing alarm, but there also was increasing tension between the British and the Indians in their own relationship. Thus, the conference was being held to determine whether these British-Indian tensions could be resolved and the French aggression stopped.

Meanwhile, Alexandrian John Carlyle had a front-row seat to observe the players, not realizing that before long, he would be a player himself.

Indians, Winchester and a Welcome Speech

To John Carlyle, the Indians must have seemed like exotic creatures. No Indians had lived in or around his hometown of Alexandria for a number of years, except possibly for a few assimilated individuals. He would have found the appearance of these Ohio Indians striking.

An Indian man would have worn a long shirt of rough cloth colored off-white that hung down from his shoulders to his thighs. He tied this shirt at the waist with a woven belt. Some men, however, wore no shirt at all, only a long cloth that passed between their legs and then looped over a belt in the front and back. Covering their thighs and calves were high leather leggings worn for protection from brush and thorns as they walked through the woods. On their feet were leather moccasins.

A male Indian's head was the most striking part of his body. It contained almost no hair. He had plucked out his beard and eyebrows and most of the hair from his head, so all that remained was a long lock that hung down his back from a small spot about two inches in diameter at the back of the top of his head. This length of hair was called a scalp lock. Then, according to his tribe and personal taste, the Indian would stiffen this scalp lock into a high ruff or leave it hanging down his back and braid it.

He also would treat his ears in a surprising way. He would slit the gristly outer rim of each ear so that this rim separated from the rest of the ear, except at the very top and very bottom. Then he would stretch that outer rim with weights. Once it had been stretched sufficiently, he would wrap copper wire around it to form a semicircle that protruded back inches from the remainder of his ear. Then he would decorate this outer semicircle with glass baubles or silver bangles. Sometimes his ears would stretch so long that they had to be tied behind his head when he ran through the woods to keep them from catching on brush and branches.

The Indians who walked into Winchester that September evening had walked all the way from their villages on the faraway Ohio River. Thus, John Carlyle and the other Virginia gentlemen at once escorted their Indian guests to the place where they would stay, what the Virginia secretary of the conference referred to as the "rough-floored shell of a building formerly

Indians walking along a village street. *Florida Center for Instructional Technology.*

80	79	78	77	76	75	74	73	72	71	70	69
57	58	59	60	61	62	63	64	65	66	67	68

56	55	54	53	52	51	50	49	48	47	46	45

1	22	23	44
2	21	24	43
3	20	25	42
4	19	26	41
5	Public Lots		40
6			39
7	18	27	38
8	17	28	37
9	16	29	36
10	15	30	35
11	14	31	34
12	13	32	33

Map of Winchester, Virginia, 1752. *Winchester-Frederick County Historical Society.*

desgn'd for a church." There the Indians "stow'd away their little baggage, & settled themselves."

This shell of a church illustrated the newness of Winchester. It had become a town only nine years earlier, in 1744 (five years before Alexandria was established). It was a rough market town laid out in a grid of seven streets—four running north and south and three running east and west— that crossed each other at right angles (see map above).

As the county seat of Frederick County, it boasted a courthouse, a prison, stocks, a pillory, a ducking stool and several taverns and shops. It also had about sixty stone or log houses that one observer described as being "rather poorly built." Also, reflecting the town's newness, some of its lots still were covered with brush and trees.

Yet it was the westernmost town in Virginia, and for that reason, it had been chosen as the site of the conference.

Once the Indians were settled, Virginia's leader, Colonel Fairfax, welcomed them. In doing so, he touched on the main subject of the conference—the recent hostile actions by the French and their Indian allies that threatened both the Ohio Indians and the Virginians.

He impressed on the Indians that he was aware of the "barbarous treatment" they had received recently from the French and assured them that "the wounds you receiv'd at that time equally affected the English."

The particular "barbarous treatment" Colonel Fairfax referred to happened a little over a year earlier, in June 1752. Then, two Frenchmen and about 250 Ottawa and Chippewa warriors from the Great Lakes region traveled south to a village of the Miami tribe on the Great Miami River in western Ohio, about ninety miles north of present-day Cincinnati.

It was about nine o'clock in the morning when the French and Indians reached the Miami village. Most of the village warriors were away hunting. The remaining Miamis, mostly women, were in their cornfields. Several British traders were also in the village in and around houses and a stockade they had built there. Suddenly, with wild war cries, the French and the Indians struck.

The traders and a few of the Miamis took shelter within the stockade that surrounded a house where the traders stored their goods. But there was no source of water inside, and soon the traders and Indians there surrendered.

During the fight, one trader had been wounded in the stomach. After the surrender, the French-aligned Indians knifed him, scalped him, cut out his heart and ate it. Additionally, five British-aligned Indians had been killed. One of them was the Miami tribal leader who had led his people away from the French and into a new alliance with the British traders. For his friendliness with the English, he was known as Old Britain. For this friendliness and for his power among the Miamis, the French-aligned Indians boiled him, cut him up and ate him.

Then the French and Indian raiders left. With them they carried away six British traders as prisoners and British trade goods valued at 3,000 pounds sterling. However, the Miamis hid two other British traders. Thus, they escaped and made their way east to report to the other Ohio Indians and the Virginians what had happened.

At Winchester, when Colonel Fairfax addressed this incident, he employed the metaphorical language used by Indians on such occasions. He assured them that the Virginians were "sensible [that] you have been shedding tears since for the loss of your friends." He held in his hand a string of wampum. Continuing, he offered the wampum to the Indians, saying that with this string he was "wiping the tears from their eyes."

Strings and belts of wampum. *National Archives.*

Fairfax then acknowledged that the Indians were tired after their long journey and gave them another string of wampum "to cheer your hearts, to open your eyes and ears, that you may see the sun clear, & hear what your brother [Virginia] has to say to you."

Wampum consisted of white or black beads, the white generally made from sea conch shells and the black (or purple) made from mussel shells. These beads were strung on a rawhide string. At times, several strings of wampum were woven into a broad belt. At the Winchester Conference, wampum was given by both Virginians and Indians as a sign of the importance and sincerity of what was being said. As one modern historian has written, with Indians, "nothing of importance was done or said without wampum."

After Fairfax finished speaking, it was the Indians' turn to reply. Their leader responded to Fairfax and the other Virginians, thanking them for their welcome and adding that he hoped Fairfax, as the governor's representative, would "open his heart & express his mind freely & not keep anything concealed therein."

When the Indian leader had concluded this short speech, the Virginians ordered wine and rum, and both the Virginians and the Indians drank good health and prosperity to each other. The Virginians made sure the Indians were served a good supper, and they then departed, as each group wished the other a good night. Then, each group began its serious preparation for the next day, the real beginning of the conference.

Conference's First Day

The following morning, the Virginians and the Indians gathered in the Frederick County Court House to begin the conference.

As with the welcoming speeches the night before, the speeches that day and for the remainder of the conference were translated by Andrew Montour and recorded by an unknown Virginian. Montour, the interpreter, was one-half of a rough-edged Lone Ranger and Tonto pair who had been for some time the principal intermediaries between the British colonists and the Ohio Indians in the wilderness.

John Carlyle must have found Montour a startling person. He was the son of a distinguished French Canadian mother and an Iroquois warrior. A description of Montour by a colonial Moravian missionary vividly indicates his mixed heritage: "He wore a brown broadcloth coat, a scarlet… waistcoat [vest], breeches over which a shirt hung…shoes, stockings, and a hat." On the other hand, his face was "encircled with a broad band of paint, applied with bear's fat," and "his ears were hung with pendants of brass and other wires plaited together like the handle of a basket." Regardless of his looks, he was much valued. He spoke fluent English, French and several Indian dialects.

The other half of this rough wilderness pair was George Croghan, who also was present in the courthouse in Winchester, there as an adviser to Colonel Fairfax. An Irishman from Dublin, he was a superb talker, speaking with a strong Irish brogue. Charming, good-natured and generous, he had become a great favorite of the Indians and even was trusted by hard-headed Philadelphia merchants, who supplied him with trade goods for the Ohio Indians. As a result, Croghan had developed an extensive trading business throughout the Ohio Country. A contemporary referred to him as an "idol among his Countrymen, the Irish Traders," and a modern historian calls him "King of the Traders."

The delegates. *Paramount Press, Inc./Robert Griffing.*

Advised by Croghan and translated by Montour, Colonel Fairfax began to speak that day. Fairfax was then sixty-two years old. No longer the land agent for the vast acreage of his cousin Lord Fairfax, he now traveled from his magnificent home, Belvoir, in Fairfax County to Williamsburg, where he served as a senior member of the Governor's Council. He had, however, only limited experience dealing with Indians and needed Croghan's counsel.

In his address to the Ohio Indians that morning of the first day of the conference at Winchester, Fairfax referred to a conference that the Virginians and the Ohio Indians held the year before in the Indian village called Logstown, located on the Ohio River about a dozen miles west of the Forks of the Ohio, Monongahela and Allegheny Rivers (where present-day Pittsburgh is located). At that conference, as Fairfax related, the Indians asked the Virginians to build "a strong house" at the Forks "where a quantity of powder, lead, etc. might be lodged to supply you [the Indians] upon an emergency" and to serve as "a place of defense, where your women & children may shelter themselves in times of danger." He now assured the Indians that such a house would be built at the Forks. He further said that he would "immediately order a quantity of powder, lead, & flints" for their guns to be sent out to the Forks. To confirm what he said, he presented the Indians with a belt of wampum.

The Indians indicated they would respond the next day. The first day of the conference then ended.

LOGSTOWN CONFERENCE PRECEDENT

At the Indian conference at Logstown the year before that Fairfax referred to, the Virginians had four main goals. First, they wanted to renew their friendship with the Ohio Indians, and they did so in part by offering them a present of trade goods (muskets, ammunition, powder, shirts, knives, scissors, etc.). Second, they wanted the Indians to agree that the Virginians could build a strong house in the Indian country to store trade goods securely. Third, they wanted an agreement to settle British families alongside the strong house. Lastly, they wanted the Indians to confirm the Virginians' right to lands in the Ohio Country, as had been alluded to in an earlier treaty.

At the Logstown Conference, they were only partially successful. The Indians pledged their continued friendship and agreed about the strong house but were uncertain about allowing a group of British colonials to settle on any of their lands and were ambiguous about an agreement concerning a British right to lands in the Ohio Country.

Yet confirming the right of the Virginians to those lands and, in particular, the right to settle on them was a key goal of the Virginians at the Logstown Conference and now at the Winchester Conference. Several years earlier, John Carlyle, Colonel Fairfax and other northern Virginians had formed the Ohio Company, and the British king had granted that company five hundred thousand acres in the Ohio Country. The company, the king and all Virginians wanted the Indians to confirm this grant and allow British settlements in the Ohio Country; the company wanted to sell land to the new settlers, and the king and other British colonists wanted a buffer of settlers between the French and French-aligned Indians and the established, well-settled areas of Pennsylvania and Virginia.

For Virginia's governor, Robert Dinwiddie, settlement of the Ohio Country was a key goal. Dinwiddie wanted to prove himself a loyal and effective servant of the king. Also, he, too, had invested in the Ohio Company.

Fairfax, Dinwiddie and the other Virginians hoped that now, at Winchester, the Indians would not only renew their vow of friendship in the face of the increased French menace but also acknowledge unambiguously that Virginians had a right to settle on Ohio lands.

However, Fairfax had not mentioned either settlements or land grants in his first address to the Indians.

SECOND DAY

The next morning at the courthouse, Scaroudy, also known as Monacatoocha, a chief of the Oneida tribe, rose and responded for the Ohio Indians.

The Oneidas were one of the six tribes that made up the Iroquois Confederacy. Although the Iroquois Confederacy was centered in upstate New York, it claimed control over the Indians in Ohio and had appointed Scaroudy as one of its representatives to the Ohio Indians. Somewhat advanced in age, he claimed to have fought in thirty-one battles, killed seven warriors and taken eleven prisoners. Because he was an Iroquois representative and an impressive warrior, as well as a forceful orator, the Ohio Indians deferred to him as their leader at the Conference.

Scaroudy opened by saying, "Our country is much disturbed at this time by the invasion of the French army; no such thing ever happened between you and us." Then, as was the custom of the Indians at conferences with the British, Scaroudy recited the metaphorical story of the beginning of the Indian-British friendship:

> *The first time the British came among us: we took hold of their ship &*
> *tied it to the grass but fearing the grass might break, removed the ship*
> *& tied her with an iron chain to a big mountain* [referring to the
> Iroquois Confederacy]. *But their brethren* [the British] *telling them*
> *their iron chain might take rust, they then tied her with a silver chain*
> *which has ever remained bright & never contracted rust. We made a strict*

In the Court House at Winchester.
Wednesday 12th Sept. 1753.
Present
The Honble William Fairfax Comiss:
The Rt Honble Thomas Lord Fairfax.
&
Gentlemen as Yesterday

Monacatoocha, addressing himself to the Comis-sioner, repeated over the first Speech deliver'd Yesterday, & gave Thanks for the same. ~ He then repeated over the Second Speech, and likewise gave Thanks for the Governor's Care of all their People,& further said, they had prepar'd a Speech in An-swer, which being accordingly deliver'd, & interpreted by Mr. Montour was as follows.~

Brother Assaraquoa

"We take this Opportunity You, that our Country is much disturb'd at this Time, by the Invasion of the French Army; no such Thing ever happned between You & Us. We remember from the First Time the English came amongst Us. We took hold of their Ship & tied it to the Grass but fearing the Grass might break, re-

[p53]

A page from the conference minutes. *Author's Collection/Library of Congress.*

alliance with our brethren the English & became one people, one heart, & one flesh; and those who draw the blood of one, must equally hurt us all.

He then said specifically: "Now brother [Virginia], harken to what I am going to say." The Frenchman "talks to us with two tongues, & we know he has two hearts." Scaroudy said the Indians knew the French wanted Indian land and did not want the English to have it. On the other hand, he knew also that the British wanted the Indians to take care of their land and not let the French have it.

Scaroudy then made his main point: "Now brother I let you know, that your kings have nothing to do with our lands; for we, the warriors fought for our lands, & so the right belongs to us, & we will take care of them." He said clearly: "Now we request you not to build the strong house, for we intend to keep our country clear of settlements during these troublesome times." He then gave a belt of wampum.

Then, attempting to soften the blow, he urged the Virginians "not to take anything amiss" from what he had just said. He still greatly desired that "the chain of friendship, so long subsisting between us, be preserved bright and free from rust." With this second statement, Scaroudy gave another belt of wampum. He then sat down.

The conference adjourned uneasily. It was the end of the second day.

THINGS CHANGED

This speech must have come as something of an unwelcome surprise to Fairfax. The Indians had reversed their stand on the strong house and clearly had no interest in giving the Virginians any right to settle anyone on their lands or any right to their lands at all.

For the Indians, things had changed since the Logstown Conference the year before. For one thing, they knew that when the French and their allied Indians raided and killed the Miamis, a strong house in the Miami village, where traders stored their trade goods and took shelter, had not prevented the massacre. In fact, friendliness toward the British may have brought on the attack.

Even worse, however, only a few months before the Winchester Conference, the French had begun to build a line of forts that they told the Indians would extend eventually from Lake Erie south down the Allegheny

River to the Ohio. In fact, by the time of the Winchester Conference, French soldiers already had completed one fort and were almost finished with a second located on a shallow creek leading from Lake Erie to the upper Allegheny River. Clearly, these forts manned by French soldiers were meant both to threaten the Indians and to keep British traders, whom the Indians depended on for many necessities, out of the Ohio Country. The Indians suspected that their agreement at Logstown allowing the Virginians to build a strong house had caused the French to rush to build their own forts first.

Thus, the Indians saw themselves as caught in the middle of two French forces. West of them were those French and Indians raiding from Canada down into the Miami territory in western Ohio, and east of them were the French soldiers building forts down the Allegheny and into the Ohio Country. In addition, they suspected that their allegiance with the British was a cause of their current troubles, and they were unsure what to do about the British.

During the summer, before the Winchester Conference, the Ohio Indians, greatly disturbed by the actions of the French, called a conference of their own people to discuss what to do.

At that conference, the Ohio Indians decided to send the Half King, another Iroquois leader, to the French who were building the forts down the Allegheny and demand they leave the Indians' lands. At the same time, they sent Scaroudy to the Virginians and, later, the Pennsylvanians to give them a similar message.

With the British colonists, however, Scaroudy had to be more delicate than the Half King with the French. The Ohio Indians still wanted British trade goods, which generally were cheaper and of better quality than the French goods, and now, most importantly, they wanted very much to preserve the option of having British help against the French.

THIRD DAY

The morning following Scaroudy's surprising speech, the conference resumed.

In a sense, this day was an anticlimax. It was the day for Colonel Fairfax, on behalf of Virginia, to address each tribe individually and urge them to maintain their friendship with the British, which he did.

An Indian speaking for his tribe. *Library of Congress*.

In response, individual tribes addressed the Virginians. Big Kettle spoke for the Wayondotts, Turtle for the Miamis and Tomenbuck for the Shawnees, each saying they would "hold fast to the chain of friendship" and each giving the Virginians a belt of wampum.

No response was made by the Virginians to Scaroudy's speech of the day before.

FOURTH DAY

On the following morning, it was learned, in the words of the official report: "The Indians, having drunk too freely last night of spirituous liquors, whereby they were much intoxicated...[were] unfit for business in the day." In consequence, it was agreed that they would wait until seven o'clock in the evening to meet.

Actually, many Indians never seemed to have learned to drink moderately. As a colonial English parson observed: "When they can get spirits, such as rum, from the English, they will always drink to excess…but they do not much care for [it] unless they can have enough to make them drunk."

When that time for the evening meeting came, the Indians and Virginians met, not at the courthouse this time but at William Cooke's Tavern, which was a surprising place given the Indians' overindulgence the night before. Apparently, however, it was where the Virginians were staying and convenient for them.

Colonel Fairfax again spoke for the Virginians. Yet he was limited by his instructions from Governor Dinwiddie and the Virginia Council. Dinwiddie, in turn, was hampered by the fact that he had not yet received instructions from London on how to respond to the new French aggression.

Dinwiddie was aware of the valuable opportunity the situation presented for the British to help the Indians keep the French out of their land and secure their loyalty. He knew, as Scaroudy had just said in Winchester, that the Indians were "much disturbed by the invasion of the French army." One of the more trustworthy Indian traders had written Governor Dinwiddie on the trader's recent return from visiting the Indians in the Ohio Country:

> The eyes of all the Indians are fixed upon you. You have it now in your power with a small expence to save this whole country for His Majesty, but if the opportunity is missed, it will never by in the power of the English to recover it but by a great expence & the united force of all the colonies.….Now is our time, if we manage well all the Indians may be brought to joining [us] against the French, otherwise, they will join the French against the English.

Dinwiddie also saw clearly the threat posed by the French. Yet France and Great Britain were at peace. In mid-June, he had written London explaining the situation, stating his concern "that the French should at this time attempt in a hostile manner to invade the King of Great Britain's dominions [that is, the Ohio Country] and [His] subjects." He asked for instructions, stating, "I hope you will think it necessary to prevent the French taking possession of the lands on the Ohio, so contiguous to our settlements." He also proposed "the absolute necessity of having two forts built on the Ohio to support His Majesty's just rights to those lands, protect our trade, and indeed support and defend our present possessions." He also recommended that London send him twenty cannons with powder and shot to arm the forts.

At the time of the Winchester Conference, however, Dinwiddie had not yet had a response from London, other than a letter saying the matter had been "laid before His Majesty." Thus, he felt, as he wrote the Governor of Pennsylvania, that "my hands are tied up, and without new Instructions I cannot act in the [forceful] Method I think necessary." Thus, he limited his instructions to Fairfax.

Fairfax, working within these limits, reminded the Indians of the large present of trade goods the governor of Virginia had sent them the year before (which included muskets, powder, bullets and flints for the guns). He then gave them a smaller amount of goods, saying he had not realized so many Indians would come as did and promising the governor would provide them a much larger quantity this coming May, some eight months away. He then ceremoniously presented the Indians with a belt of wampum.

After these remarks, Fairfax simply wished the Indians "a good journey and a safe arrival into your own country where you may find your families in perfect health and safety." Again, he failed to mention anything about a settlement of colonists, a grant of land or a strong house, much less a fort, cannons or the support of British soldiers.

Scaroudy thanked Fairfax for the presents and the speeches. Then "drinking a glass of wine each bid the other good night," and the late meeting adjourned.

LAST DAY

The next day was to be the last of the conference. The day opened with a speech by Turtle, leader of the Miamis. He solemnly assured the Virginians that his nation was firmly on the side of the British and presented them with a string of wampum painted green, saying he would "make our road…as green as this string of wampum that we may travel on a pleasant road to visit our brethren the English whenever they please to call us together." He also presented the Virginians with a council pipe with the wish that whenever they smoked it, they would remember their friendship. Finally, he presented two beaver blankets to the Virginians to show there was no deceit in their hearts.

Then the principal leader, Scaroudy, rose to speak with a belt of black wampum in his hand, indicating the seriousness of his words. Apparently, the Indians had held a further council among themselves about their final words. Possibly, also, there had been some off-the-record contacts with the Virginians, perhaps at a time when copious quantities of rum were served and consumed. At any rate, the Indians had changed their minds about having a British strong house in their country.

Scaroudy reiterated what he had said earlier about not wanting Virginians to settle on their lands "at this troublesome time" and about the Indians' intention to "drive the French away quite out of our country."

Then he pointed to interpreter Andrew Montour and two Virginia traders and said he wanted them appointed as intermediaries between his people and the Virginians. He requested Virginia to send immediately to the Indians in the Ohio Country by those intermediaries a supply of powder and bullets for use by his warriors "to defend ourselves against our enemies." When these goods arrived in the Ohio Country, the Indians then would "show them a place where the strong house shall be built to store those things for our use." So saying, he presented the valuable belt to the Virginians.

Scaroudy had asked for help from the Virginians, as the trader who wrote to Dinwiddie had predicted. Surprisingly, however, Colonel Fairfax did not respond, at least not for the record. Thus, the meeting adjourned.

DAY OF REST

The following day was Sunday. Many of the Indians attended a sermon given at the courthouse by a local minister and, according to the official report, "behaved decently."

In the afternoon, Scaroudy and his wife brought their only son, who was about eleven years old, to the courthouse to be christened. Colonel Fairfax and one of the Indian traders stood as godfathers, and the boy was given the name Dinwiddie.

Then a chief called Delaware George and his wife presented their infant daughter for baptism, and Colonel Fairfax named her Sarah (after his daughter, John Carlyle's wife). Lastly, the interpreter Andrew Montour presented an eighteen-year-old kinsman, who was baptized John. Then, the official report recorded, on "drinking a glass of wine & wishing much happiness to the parents, & the new Christians, each departed with joy in their countenances."

The next day, the Indians took their leave.

POSTSCRIPT

At the end of the official report and after the Indians left, Colonel Fairfax wrote an odd postscript addressed to Governor Dinwiddie. In it, Fairfax admitted that the Indians had not confirmed the earlier grant of lands to Virginia. He wrote, however, that the Indian leaders had told him privately that they had not done so because there were two French-aligned Indian spies in their delegation and the Indian leaders were afraid the spies would report them as being too friendly with the British if they confirmed the grant.

Fairfax continued that he did not want to offend the Indians' sensitivity on this point, so "I did not care to touch on that subject [of the grant]" publicly. Fairfax concluded lamely that he was sure this setback was only temporary. He wrote, "I doubt not when your honour meets them next year, they will cheerfully & faithfully confirm the said lands to His Majesty."

This postscript is an admission that Fairfax had failed in one of his primary missions, getting the grant of land to Virginia confirmed. Also, though he may not have realized it, in it, he indicated that the Indians' support of the British against the French was weak. If they were reluctant for the French even to learn they had been too friendly with the Virginians, how strong would they be in the future to give the British vigorous and wholehearted support against the French?

POST-CONFERENCE MANEUVERS

After the conference, events moved quickly. As planned, Scaroudy and the Ohio Indians met the Pennsylvanians at Carlisle, Pennsylvania, in early October. There, they received much the same friendly but cautious reception they had received in Virginia. While there, however, they also received some bad news. The other half of their diplomatic effort, the visit of the Half King to the French, had been a disaster. Not only had the French refused to stop building forts, but the commander of the French forts had also insulted the Half King, calling him "an Old Woman." As for the belt of wampum the Half King had ritually presented him, the French commander flung it back to him while dismissing all Indians as "Flies, or Musquitos."

Scaroudy and his group of Ohio Indians quickly returned home to the Ohio Country to consult with the Half King on their next moves. Would they support the French or the British? The answer is in the next chapter, "A Huge, Red Bull's Eye."

As for John Carlyle, he was not finished with the French and Indians—or the British. That, too, is related in the next chapter.

Chapter 4

"A HUGE, RED BULL'S EYE"

George Washington at General Braddock's Defeat

I n 1755, a British army commanded by Major General Edward
Braddock of the Coldstream Guards marched along a rough wilderness
road in western Pennsylvania. Riding his horse at the front, Captain
Harry Gordon, a military engineer, saw movement among the trees ahead.
Abruptly, a British scout burst out of the woods and onto the road, running
flat out toward him; another followed.

Gordon reined in his horse as the first scout reached him. As Gordon later
wrote, the scout reported that "a Considerable Body of the Enemy…were
at hand." Gordon glanced up where the scout had been and saw, much to
his surprise, dozens of Indians and French soldiers on the road ahead and in
the woods between the trees, running straight at him. Leading them was a
Frenchman dressed like an Indian.

Thus began the Battle of the Monongahela, one of the worst defeats in
the history of the British army. There to experience the defeat firsthand
was young, ambitious George Washington, one of Braddock's aides. Also
with Braddock were two future generals in opposing armies—Thomas Gage
of the British army and Daniel Morgan of the not-yet-existent American
Continental army. Back in the line of march, driving one of Braddock's
supply wagons, was future frontiersman Daniel Boone. And another colonist,
Benjamin Franklin, had helped the army get supplies and transportation.
Despite the roles these men would play in the future, not one of them
imagined at the time that this battle would lead to a much bigger conflict
twenty years later—the American Revolution.

George Washington. *Washington and Lee University, University Collections of Art and History.*

THE BEGINNING OF THE CONFLICT

The story of the fight began much earlier, in the 1500s, when French fur trappers and black-robed Jesuit priests paddled up the St. Lawrence River west from the Atlantic Ocean to the Great Lakes, seeking beaver to trap and Indian souls to save. From the Great Lakes, French gold seekers and adventurers headed south down the Mississippi River to the Gulf of Mexico. As they traveled, the French established widely separated settlements near the riverbanks. Most were little more than trading posts, but they included Quebec and New Orleans.

The British, however, settled North America in different areas from the French and in very different ways. These Anglo settlers were mainly farmers and merchants, and from the Atlantic seaboard south of the St. Lawrence, they spread steadily westward, covering the land with bustling towns and farms with plowed fields.

Meanwhile, in the deep forests between the French trading posts and the British towns were Indians. Led by the Six Nations of the Iroquois, the northeastern tribes usually remained more or less unified in support of one or the other of these new groups of settlers. Farther west and south, the Indians generally were fragmented into separate tribes that disagreed about the Europeans. The loyalty of a tribe, such as the Shawnee, might shift back and forth between the British and French according to who offered the best trading goods, who was more likely to win the next battle or who would help keep the other power away from the tribe's lands. Gradually, however, many Indians began to realize that the French were few and transient, while the British were numerous and, when they came, they came to stay.

The farther west a man traveled from the Atlantic, the more uncertain were the boundaries between the British and the French colonies. At first, this uncertainty made little difference—a lot of wilderness lay between the arc of water stretching from Quebec to New Orleans and the towns in Pennsylvania and Virginia.

By the 1740s, however, Virginians and Pennsylvanians began to eye the lands farther west in the Ohio River valley. Some of the most prominent men in Virginia formed the Ohio Company in 1747, and in 1749, they persuaded King George II to grant them a large tract of land in the Ohio Valley. By then, Pennsylvania traders had penetrated the Ohio Valley, offering the Indians cheap British-manufactured goods in exchange for furs.

The French also claimed that land and considered it vital to their fur trade and communication routes. Under a new governor, the Marquis Ange Duquesne de Menneville, they began building a series of forts from Lake Erie to the Ohio River to keep the British colonists out.

Virginians Respond

At first, the Virginians responded with diplomacy. In 1753, they sent twenty-one-year-old George Washington to one of the new French forts to convey their claim to the French in writing. To the Virginians, Washington's credentials were excellent. He was half-brother of a founder of the Ohio Company, and as a surveyor for the vast lands of the Fairfax family, he had become an experienced woodsman. For his part, Washington was eager to prove he could handle a delicate mission for his country. But Washington spoke no French and had no diplomatic experience at all.

The French were unimpressed and continued building.

The next year, the acting royal governor of Virginia (a partner in the Ohio Company) made young Washington a lieutenant colonel in the Virginia militia and sent him back to the Ohio River with a small number of militiamen. Washington was ordered to begin building forts and "restrain… or kill & destroy" anyone who interfered.

After their deliberations, mentioned in the last chapter, the Half King, Scaroudy and other Ohio Indians decided that it was in their best interests to support the British, who now seemed to be determined to drive the French away. Thus, the Half King and a small group of Ohio Indians joined Washington as he advanced.

But Washington also had little military experience, and this venture also failed, miserably. The French and their Indian allies surrounded Washington and his soldiers in their hastily constructed Fort Necessity at Great Meadows in southwestern Pennsylvania and forced them to capitulate. On July 4, 1754, Washington and his men evacuated the fort and returned to Virginia.

Just before the battle, the Half King and his warriors, apparently unimpressed with Washington and foreseeing the battle's outcome, left Washington and disappeared into the woods. A few months afterward, the Half King died.

The failed Washington venture had two immediate effects: it strengthened the French position with the Ohio Indians, and it led the Virginians to appeal to London for regular army troops to drive the French out of the valley. In England at the same time, the Duke of Cumberland, the King's second son, led a government faction seeking an excuse for another war with France. (Britain and France had fought each other in three major wars that had lasted much of the previous sixty-five years.) Now French actions in the Ohio Valley gave them an excuse.

Enter the British Army

General Braddock. *Alamy.*

The British evolved a plan that began with an attack on the French Fort Duquesne, located in a small wilderness clearing at the confluence of the Allegheny, Monongahela and Ohio Rivers (site of present-day Pittsburgh). The duke, a former member of the Coldstream Guards, chose sixty-year-old Major General Edward Braddock of the guards to lead the expedition.

The portly Braddock had forty-five years of military service, most of it spent in London as an officer of the elite St. James Palace Guard. There he inspected sentries and ordered drummers to beat a salute whenever a member of the royal family passed through the palace gate. This duty taught him how to impose discipline and present a good appearance but no other valuable military skills. Not once in all his years of service had Braddock led troops in combat. During numerous spirited conversations in guardrooms, taverns and clubs, however, Braddock had acquired the British army's unquestioned belief that British soldiers led by a fearless British officer formed the best fighting force in the world, and he was dismissive of any military body composed of lesser mortals.

In early March 1755, Braddock and his soldiers sailed up the Potomac River in seventeen ships and arrived at Alexandria, Virginia. Alexandria today is a city of some 155,000 people just down the Potomac River from Washington, D.C., but in 1755 it consisted mainly of several bare wooden buildings strung along a few dirt streets. The British soldiers were not pleased—Alexandria had no coffeehouse, no pastry shop, no brothel and only one or two small taverns.

Braddock established his headquarters in the largest building in the village, merchant John Carlyle's new white stone house. As his soldiers were unimpressed with the small Virginia town, Braddock was unimpressed with the Virginia troops, who, in their blue uniforms (to the extent they had uniforms), now joined the red-coated British troops.

Braddock had the Virginians drilled over and over again in the dust of Market Square, across the street from his headquarters. The Virginians would form up shoulder to shoulder, wheel around by whole platoons and fire—a maneuver proper to spacious, treeless European battlefields but less useful in the dense woods where they were headed.

Braddock's troops landing at West's Point in Alexandria. *Patrick O'Brien/Hal Hardaway*.

Although far from dazzled by the colonials, Braddock was impressed with one Virginian—the young George Washington, who came from nearby Mount Vernon to meet the major general at Carlyle's house to seek a position in Braddock's army. Braddock saw a tall, lean, reddish-brown-haired veteran of the earlier conflict with the French and Indians in the same forests where he planned to take his army. Braddock offered Washington a voluntary position as one of his aides.

Washington wanted a commission in the regular British army, but Braddock lacked the power to grant one. Even though the position Braddock offered meant he would not have the dignity of being paid, Washington could not miss the opportunity to be part of the largest British army yet to appear in Virginia. He quickly accepted the post, and he began hand-copying for future study all orders Braddock had issued since his arrival in Virginia.

At the same time, another provincial officer—whose offer of help Braddock curtly rejected—was Richard Henry Lee of the prominent Lee family of Virginia. Twenty-one years later, on June 7, 1776, Lee stood before the Second Continental Congress and introduced a resolution beginning, "Resolved, That these United Colonies are, and of right ought to be, free and independent," which soon was expanded to become the Declaration of Independence.

Reenactment of General Braddock greeting colonial governors at John Carlyle's House. *Author's collection.*

Then, on April 14 and for the next two days, there was held at John Carlyle's house the largest assembly of royal governors ever convened in the colonies. The meeting's purpose was for the governors of Maryland, Pennsylvania, New York, Massachusetts and Virginia to discuss with General Braddock military and financial strategy.

At the conference, Braddock presented the governors a plan developed in London for the campaign against the French and the Indians. The exceedingly ambitious plan included not only Braddock's attack on Fort Duquesne but also attacks on French forts on Lake Ontario and Lake Champlain and in Nova Scotia—all paid for from a common fund established by the colonial assemblies.

The governors agreed with the military plan, but they reported they had been unable to persuade their assemblies to agree to a common fund. Further, they said that if the fund were to be created, Parliament must create it and must assess each colony to fund it. In effect, they proposed that Parliament tax the colonies. (Ten years later, it did—when it passed the Stamp Act, which the colonies despised.)

Angered, Braddock urged the governors to press their assemblies further for funds and supplies. Reluctantly, the governors agreed, and on April 16, the conference adjourned.

Braddock Begins His March

Meanwhile, in early April, Braddock's army had begun leaving Alexandria for the British base camp at Fort Cumberland (now Cumberland, Maryland) more than 175 miles away.

The Alexandrians, for their part, were glad to see the British go. "They used us like an enemy country," John Carlyle wrote later. "Took everything they wanted and paid nothing or very little for it. When complaints were made to the Commanding Officers, they curst the country and inhabitants calling us the spawn of Convicts, the sweepings of the jail, etc."

When Braddock left Alexandria, he still needed provisions, wagons and horses to complete his long march successfully. He expected both that the colonial governments of Pennsylvania and Maryland would provide the provisions and that what he needed would be waiting for him in Frederick, Maryland, a small frontier town near the Pennsylvania border. But earlier, Braddock had bluntly berated the Pennsylvania Assembly for its "pusillanimous and improper Behavior" because of what he considered its miserly attitude toward his expedition. When Braddock reached Frederick, his quartermaster told him the locals had provided nothing.

Fortunately for Braddock, a visiting Pennsylvania assemblyman named Benjamin Franklin was in Frederick. Franklin offered his services and immediately printed broadsides offering a fair price for horses and wagons and had the broadsides distributed in nearby Pennsylvania counties. Franklin let it be known that if in two weeks no wagons and horses were forthcoming for pay, they would be taken without recompense.

Braddock got the transportation for his supplies. For himself, he did even better. He left Frederick on May 1 riding in a fancy chariot provided by the governor of Maryland. Just after passing through Winchester, Virginia, Braddock rode by his troops in style while they, with their cannons and heavy wagons, struggled in the mud. They finally reached Fort Cumberland on May 10. It took Braddock almost a full month to gather additional supplies, so the main body of his army did not begin to leave Fort Cumberland until June 7. Its objective, Fort Duquesne, was still more than one hundred miles away.

Braddock's troops marching toward Fort Duquesne. *Author's collection.*

By then, Braddock's force consisted of about 2,150 fighting men: British regulars, colonials, a detachment of sailors to fire siege cannons borrowed from English ships at Alexandria and a handful of frontiersmen and Indian scouts. (Scaroudy and a few of his followers went with him, as did Montour, the interpreter at the Winchester Conference, and Croghan, Fairfax's former adviser at the Conference.) Also going along were soldiers' wives and wagon drivers (including twenty-year-old Daniel Boone and rugged eighteen-year-old Daniel Morgan, later the victorious Continental army general in command at the Revolutionary War's Battle of Cowpens). The going was rough and slow as they marched along a narrow trail through dense forests, across river and over mountains—all through hostile Indian lands. After nine days on the trail, the expedition had gone only twenty-two miles, an average of two and a half miles per day.

At this point, Braddock heard that French reinforcements were moving south from Canada toward Fort Duquesne. For greater speed, and partly on the advice of Washington, he decided to divide his troops. Taking an advance party of 1,200 to 1,300 of the best men, he hurried on ahead, leaving the bulk of his supplies and the remainder of his men to come later.

THE ADVANCE PARTY PROCEEDS

As the advance party proceeded, the men became aware that they were being watched. At daybreak on July 6, British grenadiers found three bloody corpses—British soldiers, shot and scalped. Within minutes, every man in the expedition knew what had happened. American frontiersmen with the army had grimly warned of the "scalping and mohawking" and other "barbarous usage" a soldier could expect if he fell among the Indians. This awareness later led to another unfortunate incident. Scaroudy's son, who had been christened Dinwiddie at Winchester, was returning from a scouting party ahead of the main body of troops when the now-nervous British soldiers took him for a French-aligned Indian, fired on him and killed him.

Three days later, about one o'clock in the afternoon on July 9, the advance party had completed a dangerous crossing of the wide, shallow Monongahela River. Once safely on the other side, it was less than ten miles from the French fort.

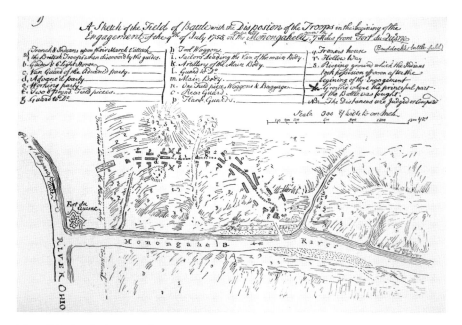

Map of the battle site. *mapsofpa.com.*

Braddock had formed the advance party into roughly three groups: a vanguard of half his men preceded by a handful of scouts; the main body, composed of Braddock and his staff (including Washington), Braddock's guard of regulars, some Virginians and all the wagons (one driven by Boone) with provisions and baggage; and finally, a small rear guard, almost all Americans. Braddock chose as his commander of the vanguard Lieutenant Colonel Thomas Gage, who twenty years later, as General Gage, would command all British forces in North America. At this point, the wagons and numerous men left behind weeks earlier were some fifty miles to the rear of the advance party—much too far to help in an attack.

Braddock and his soldiers marched along a rough wilderness road surrounded by forest with a wooded hill rising to their right. It was there that the Frenchman dressed like an Indian suddenly came running at Harry Gordon, and the fight began.

THE BATTLE

The Frenchman, forty-four-year-old Canadian-born Captain Daniel Hyacinthe Marie Lienard de Beaujeu, was not alone. Behind him were roughly 250 French Canadian regulars and militiamen and 600 Indians from Fort Duquesne—about two-thirds the fighting men Braddock had. Beaujeu had planned to ambush the British as they crossed the river. Not realizing he was too late, he and his French Canadian and Indian force were rushing from the fort toward the river when they ran right into the British. Each group saw the other at the same time.

As Gage's front rank of grenadiers began to form up, Beaujeu, who was running with his hat in his hand, stopped, raised the hat and began to wave it from side to side above his head. Immediately, with a wild, raw yell, the Indians—Potawatomis, Wyandots, Ottawas, Shawnees and Mingos—running behind him parted to the left and right into the woods and vanished. At the same time, some French Canadian soldiers hurriedly formed a line stretching across the road in front of the British vanguard.

In good order, Gage's troops formed two lines facing the French—front line kneeling, back line standing—and fired their muskets. The volley killed Beaujeu and unnerved his soldiers. The Indians, however, were untouched.

Left: A French Canadian soldier. *Canadian War Museum*.

Right: Painted for war. *Paramount Press, Inc./Robert Griffing*.

Indians attacking. *Library of Congress.*

Many of the British were hearing the Indians' harrowing war cries for the first time as the warriors "swarmed through the forest along both flanks of the English, hid behind trees, bushes, and fallen trunks, or crouched in gullies and ravines, and opened deadly fire on the helpless soldiers, who, themselves completely visible, could see no enemy, and wasted volley after volley on the impassive trees," wrote the expressive nineteenth-century historian Francis Parkman.

The British vanguard quickly lost many of its officers, singled out as they rode their horses and waved their swords, and began a fighting retreat. Within a few paces, however, the soldiers of the vanguard ran into most of the main force as it advanced at Braddock's order.

The two groups collided in the powder smoke and terrifying noise, creating a large, disorganized mass in the middle of the narrow road. Confused redcoats bumped into each other, swore and looked for space to stand and shoot—or for someone to hide behind. "The men were sometimes 20 or 30 deep," later wrote a British officer, "and he thought himself securest who was in the Center."

To the Indians on both sides of the road, the bunched-up soldiers presented, as one observer noted, a "huge, red bull's eye" that the warriors fired into with bloody effect.

Braddock rode his horse into the middle of his rattled soldiers and tried to direct them into battle lines and advance. He had little success. The Virginians among them, meanwhile, had begun to fan out individually and in small groups to fight more effectively from behind trees like the Indians.

The Virginians' actions, however, clashed with Braddock's intense sense of courage and discipline—and his earlier instructions—and he was furious. He "stormed much, calling them Cowards," a British officer remembered, "and even went so far as to strike them with his own Sword for attempting the Trees."

Still, a few American colonists dashed to a large fallen tree lying in the woods nearer the Indians and opened fire. The British regulars, seeing the smoke from the American muskets and their blue coats and buckskin, mistook them for French Canadians and shot and killed several, forcing the rest to rejoin the British troops. Few Americans attempted to reach the woods again.

Serving as Braddock's aide during the battle, Washington had no troops under his command. However, early in the fight, Braddock's two other aides were shot, and it fell to Washington to distribute the general's orders. As

Wounding of General Braddock. *Paramount Press, Inc./Robert Griffing.*

Washington went along the road among the few officers who remained unwounded, two horses were shot out from under him and four bullets tore holes in his coat, but miraculously, he was not hit.

Braddock, though inflexible, was no coward. Trying to organize his troops, he dashed back and forth on horseback, a prime target. Four horses were killed while he rode them. Attempting to mount a fifth, he "was wounded with a musket ball, which went thru his right arm, his side and lodged in his lungs," according to one observer. It would turn out to be a fatal wound.

All around the British, "the ground [was] strewn with dead and wounded men, the bounding of maddened horses, the clatter and roar of musketry and cannon, mixed with the spiteful report of rifles and the yells that rose from the indefatigable throats of six hundred unseen [hostile Indians]," wrote Parkman.

The soldiers, seeing most of their officers dead or wounded, an enemy facing them they could hear but not see, most of their ammunition gone and their commander down, turned and fled. "They broke and run as sheep pursued by dogs," wrote Washington later, "and it was impossible to rally them."

One British officer, who began to retreat after failing to rally his troops, later wrote, "Before I got 40 yards in the River, I turn'd about on hearing the Indians Yell, & saw them tomahawk some of our wounded people."

Daniel Boone watched as the fleeing army streamed by the supply wagons at the back of the line. Knowing the treatment he could expect if the Indians found him stuck with a heavily laden wagon, Boone jumped onto his team, cut the traces and galloped to safety to fight another day. Wily Scaroudy, Montour and Croghan also survived.

Early in the battle, Harry Gordon, who had first seen the enemy, was shot in the right arm, and he recalled that the bone shattered "half way Between the Elbow & wrist." He added that despite the pain, he "was too Anxious to allow myself to Quit the field" until he had no other choice.

Lieutenant Colonel Gage, commander of the vanguard, suffered what he describes as "a slight wound in the belly." He could not stop his soldiers either and hurried back across the Monongahela to relative safety.

Braddock's army was finished.

Opposite: Victorious! *Author's collection.*

THE BATTLE'S AFTERMATH

As the survivors straggled fifty miles back to the rear echelon, they appeared to one observer "like spirits more than men, and their wounds alive with maggots." Daniel Morgan watched them come into camp. Earlier in the expedition, the husky Morgan had been court-martialed and given a number of lashes for knocking down a British soldier who angered him. That day he heard and saw nothing to increase his respect for the British army.

The French and Indians made no serious effort to follow up their victory. Four days later, Braddock himself died farther back down the trail. Under a new commander, the regular British troops turned, not to Virginia but to the safety of crowded Philadelphia, leaving the families settled in western Maryland, Virginia and Pennsylvania unguarded against the aroused French and Indians.

It was not long before colonial newspapers in Boston, New York, Philadelphia, Annapolis, Williamsburg and Charleston reported the "melancholy Accounts," "dreadful Havoc" and "very shocking circumstances" of Braddock's defeat. The *New York Mercury* noted the resulting vulnerability of colonial frontiers and wondered "how much innocent Blood may be inhumanly sacrificed to the Cowardice of the British Soldiers." In a letter quoted in the *Virginia Gazette*, a man in New York wrote a friend in Boston, "It is generally lamented that the British Veterans were not put into Garrison, and New England Irregulars sent to Ohio."

For the first time, future revolutionaries had seen that the formidable British regular army could be defeated, even routed. In a letter to a family friend shortly after the battle, Washington wrote of Braddock's defeat, "Had I not been witness to the fact on that fatal Day, I sh'd scarce give credit to it now." Benjamin Franklin later wrote in his autobiography, "This whole Transaction [Braddock's defeat] gave us Americans the first Suspicion that our exalted Ideas for the Prowess of British Regulars had not been well founded."

Braddock's defeat was the first major confrontation in the French and Indian War. It took several years and a new prime minister for Britain to understand, in part because of the Braddock fiasco, that if it were to fight the French seriously in North America, it must use good troops, well provisioned and well led. When it did, Quebec fell, and the French colonial era in North America was largely finished.

However, winning the French and Indian War proved expensive for the British. To pay for the war, the British government imposed a series of taxes so hated by the colonists that a new commitment of British soldiers was required to enforce them.

As time passed, more and more colonists began to agree with Carlyle, the Alexandria merchant whose house had been Braddock's headquarters, that "they used us like an enemy country." With the French no longer a threat, the colonists were less willing to do as London said.

Before long, on each side of the road from Concord to Lexington, those taking cover behind trees and firing at British redcoats were neither Frenchmen nor Indians but American colonists. The general who ordered the British troops onto the road to Lexington in 1775 was Braddock's old commander of the vanguard on the road to Fort Duquesne, and Thomas Gage failed to appreciate the very serious threat posed by men fighting American-style.

The colonials had learned the lesson of Braddock's defeat—the British had not.

Chapter 5

ALEXANDRIA AND THE WAR OF 1812

The United States Declares War, 1812

On June 18, 1812, President James Madison took the nation to war. On that date, he signed a bill passed by Congress declaring that the United States was at war with Great Britain.

That war, known as the War of 1812, would have a great effect on the young United States, and particularly on the town of Alexandria, an effect not entirely what was intended. Why, then, did the young United States, on a day in June 221 years ago, go to war, for the second time, with the most powerful nation on earth? What did Alexandrians think about this war?

The declaration of war received far from unanimous support in Congress. In the House, 39 percent of congressmen opposed the war. In the Senate, 41 percent of senators were opposed.

In Alexandria, Samuel Snowden, the thirty-eight-year-old editor of the *Alexandria Gazette*, voiced Alexandria's opposition to the war. In a stinging editorial, he wondered whether Congress was "really so mad as to wish to involve us in a partial and disastrous war."

Those who favored war, led by President Madison, pointed to the grievous affront that, for years, their old enemy Great Britain had given the fledgling United States by seizing its ships (389 had been seized since November 1807) and by pressing U.S. citizens into involuntary service in the British navy. Approximately 9,990 American seamen were so impressed from 1807 to

A British officer selects American seamen aboard an American ship. *Library of Congress.*

January 1, 1812. As Madison indignantly stated in his message to Congress seeking war, "Thousands of American citizens…have been torn from their country and from everything dear to them; have been dragged on board ships of war of a foreign nation…to be exiled to the most distant and deadly climes [and] to risk their lives in the battles of their oppressors."

War supporters also pointed to the orders adopted by the royal British government and enforced by a naval blockade that arrogantly required U.S. ships to stop at a British port and pay British customs duties before entering a port on the European continent.

Great Britain took these strong measures because it was in the middle of a deadly war with Napoleonic France and badly needed ships, seamen and trade. For the United States, however, that was hardly sufficient justification for actions that grated harshly on its proud sovereignty.

In addition, western states, like Ohio and Kentucky, suspected that Great Britain had been urging Indians living in Canada and in the Indiana, Michigan and Illinois Territories to attack their communities. A Lexington, Kentucky newspaper emotionally editorialized: "The SCALPING KNIFE and TOMAHAWK of British savages, [are] now again devastating our frontiers."

Moreover, representatives from these western states, like young congressman Henry Clay of Kentucky, looked at British Canada and saw easy pickings. Why should the British control that part of North America, and not the United States? Clay asserted that the Kentucky militia by itself could easily capture Montreal and proclaimed, "I prefer the troubled ocean of war…to the tranquil, putrescent pool of ignominious peace."

On the other side, those opposing the war were concentrated mainly in the northeastern states. New England merchants, with their minds on the bottom line, thought: *So we lose a few ships and a few sailors every now and then—isn't that just the cost of doing business? Why go to war with the nation with the most powerful navy on earth? Won't war mean we lose more ships, and won't it likely bring about New England's economic collapse?* In addition, New Englanders were bothered very little by the problems of Indians in the western states. They pointed out how quiet the Indians were along their own borders.

Virginia's John Randolph was a leading opponent of the war. On the floor of the House, he asked rhetorically how the country could "go to war without money, without men, without a navy…?" (In 1812, the British navy had some 620 warships. The American navy had fewer than 20.)

Randolph may have been motivated in part by his dislike of Henry Clay. When Clay became Speaker of the House, he had ordered Randolph not to bring his hunting dogs onto the House floor as Randolph was accustomed to doing. Randolph later colorfully expressed his thoughts about Clay, describing him as "being so brilliant yet so corrupt, which like a rotten mackerel by moonlight, he shined and stunk."

Like Randolph, most Alexandrians opposed the war, following the lead of Samuel Snowden and the *Gazette*. On the day after war was declared, Snowden prophetically wrote: "While we are…beating out the brains of our unoffending neighbors in the north [in Canada], what surety have we that a diversion more horrid will not be meted to us in the south? What pledge have we that a naval force will not be sent to lay our rich maritime cities under enormous contributions, or raze them to the ground?"

He and other Alexandrians would learn that there was little surety at all.

ALEXANDRIA IN 1812

In June 1812, when the United States declared war on Great Britain and the War of 1812 began, what was Alexandria like?

Alexandria then was part of the District of Columbia and had been since 1801. In the 1810 census, its population was only 7,227 (68 percent White, 12 percent free Black and 20 percent enslaved Black). In comparison, the population of Washington proper was 8,208, only about 1,000 more than Alexandria's. (Georgetown was a separate town, population 4,948.)

According to maps developed from 1810 tax lists, the developed area of Alexandria extended no farther north than Pendleton Street and no farther south than Jefferson Street, a twelve-block area. From the Potomac River it extended west to West Street on the south side of Cameron Street and only to Fayette Street on the north side of Cameron.

Some Alexandrians lived in brick homes, but most lived in small wooden houses. When they wanted to go somewhere, they walked, or they rode over dirt or cobblestone streets on horseback or in horse-drawn carriages, coaches or wagons.

An Alexandrian walking along King Street would have heard horses' shod hooves striking cobblestones and the rattle of carriages and wagons. He or she would have smelled chimney smoke from coal and wood fires while walking past buildings whose first floors housed retail stores and top floors enclosed the living quarters of the stores' owners.

For example, walking toward the river along the south side of King Street between St. Asaph and Pitt Streets (the area now dominated by the city courthouse), an Alexandrian would have passed two three-story brick buildings built close to the sidewalk.

The first floor of the first building was occupied by John Withers & Company, selling "British, French, India, Russia and American GOODS," as advertised in the *Alexandria Gazette*. The second building was the slightly larger store and home of silversmith Adam Lynn Jr. Here, on the first floor, Lynn maintained a combination jewelry and hardware store, where he sold such goods as tea trays, swords, nails, watch chains, scissors, saddles and earrings.

As our walker proceeded down King Street, he or she might have encountered several well-dressed Alexandria men and women. This was a period of revolution in fashion. In 1812, a well-dressed man no longer wore the artificial powdered wigs, knee britches, stockings and shoes with bright buckles of George Washington. Instead, he dressed in long pants tucked into boots that rose to just below his knees. His coat was double- or single-breasted and solid colored. Its front was cut straight across along the waistline, and in back, it was cut into two tails that hung down to his knees. Under his coat, he wore a waistcoat (vest) of a different color or pattern from the outer coat, and his throat was wrapped high in a silk or muslin neckcloth. An elegant top hat completed his fashionable image.

Similarly, a well-dressed woman no longer wore side hoops or bum rolls to make her skirt look fuller. She wore instead a gown or frock made of soft

Left: Gentleman's dress in 1812. *Journal Des Dames et Des Modes, Paris.*

Right: Lady's dress in 1812. *Lady's Magazine, London.*

muslin "cinched up high just under the breasts to suggest a high waist," according to historian Daniel Pool. From the high waist (in the new Empire fashion) the gown hung straight down following the natural contours of her body to her shoe tops. Walking outdoors, she would have worn a fashionable bonnet tied under her chin.

Walking past these well-dressed men and women, our Alexandrian soon would have reached the corner of Pitt and King Streets. Directly across Pitt Street, he or she would have seen the popular Washington Tavern at the spot now occupied by a hotel, the Alexandrian. High up at the corner of the tavern was affixed a swinging sign with the likeness of General Washington on horseback painted on each side. On one side, Washington rode a bay and on the other, a dark gray. The tavern served meals and drinks, rented rooms and provided a stable and forage for horses. As our Alexandrian crossed Pitt Street, he would have caught the dank smell of the stable mixed with the enticing aroma of coffee and tobacco.

Continuing down King Street, our walker would have come to the center of Alexandria's commerce, the harbor. There, commodious warehouses stored tobacco, flour, wheat, ship's bread and other commodities waiting for shipment to American seacoast towns, the West Indies and Europe. (One such warehouse, the Fitzgerald Warehouse, still stands at 100–104 South Union Street. It now houses a Starbucks and the Old Town Shop.)

Wharves stretched out into the Potomac River from the town's shore, where ships were made secure with strong ropes. The wharves smelled of stagnant water and emitted the sharp tang of tar from ships' riggings. The week in June when war was declared, the *Alexandria Gazette* reported that fifteen ships had recently arrived in port and were tied to the wharves, including the brigs *Rising Sun* from Cuba and *Hunter* from Portugal, plus the schooner *Three Sallys* from New York and the sloop *Montezuma* from Norfolk.

That month in 1812, Alexandria presented a peaceful scene. Our walker and other Alexandrians, however, must have been uneasy about what this new war meant for them. Would ships still be able to enter and depart from their harbor and do business with distant trading partners? Could their town itself be secure from the powerful British army and British navy?

BLOCKADE AND RAIDS, 1813

During the eight months following the United States' declaration of war on Great Britain, the war had little effect on Alexandria.

Then, on February 12, 1813, the *Alexandria Gazette* reported from Norfolk that a heavily armed British navy squadron had just entered the Chesapeake Bay and that its commander had proclaimed, "The Chesapeake and all its ports, harbors and waters [are] in a state of strict and rigorous blockade." This was not an idle threat, and for the first time, war would be felt in Alexandria. Moreover, a blockade of shipping would be only part of the mission of the British navy.

The blockading squadron contained at least eight ships: two seventy-four-gun ships of the line, three frigates, a sloop of war, a brig of war and a small schooner. It was clear to Alexandrians, particularly Alexandrian shippers and merchants, that its strength was more than adequate to enforce the blockade. The British navy easily outnumbered and outgunned the warships available to the Americans to keep the channel to the sea open. In fact, the only reasonably large ship available to the Americans was the frigate

Constellation, which carried only about half the guns of one of the seventy-fours alone. The blockaders quickly rendered it useless by chasing it into Norfolk harbor.

A reader predicted in the *Gazette* on February 13 that the blockade would result in a "fall of the price of our flour and grain," key elements of Alexandria's trade. The reader continued: "At length the war is brought home to us. Yeah, it is brought home to us!"

In April, Alexandria gentlemen in top hats, tailcoats and boots eagerly gathered around the *Gazette* office on the west side of the 100 block of South Royal Street to pick up the latest edition of the paper. Possibly some gentlemen or their wives instead sent servants to the office to pick up their copies.

Regardless of how they got their papers, they read the upsetting news that British warships were now actually at the mouth of the Potomac River and had turned back a schooner from Alexandria bound for the West Indies. The schooner's captain related that the British told him that in their recent voyage in the Chesapeake Bay, they had captured several privateers from Baltimore and "taken about 3,000 barrels of flour out of small vessels, and burnt the vessels."

All this information dampened the mood of Alexandrians. The *Gazette* reported observing about town "silent streets, deserted warehouses, dismantled ships, long faces, and various other symptoms of public calamity and private grief."

Then, on May 6, the *Gazette* contained an ominous report headed "Havre-de-Grace Destroyed." According to the report, the British had bombarded the small Maryland port, located where the Susquehanna River enters the bay, "with shot, shells and rockets," and "the destruction was general." Washington's *Daily National Intelligencer*, probably brought to Alexandria on the ferry from Washington, contained a more complete, eyewitness description of Havre de Grace's destruction: "The force of the enemy consisted of six hundred men, four hundred of whom were landed in the town....They burnt twenty-four of the best houses in the town and plundered all the rest."

The *Intelligencer* also reported that the soldiers were led by Rear Admiral George Cockburn (pronounced "Coe-burn"). Later, the *Gazette* reported that a British navy deserter who had been at Havre de Grace related that Cockburn "not only led on the forces in person but took the most active and conspicuous part in the disgraceful scenes which were acted on that occasion."

This attack deeply impressed Alexandrians, and it and similar later raids would affect profoundly their behavior in the future. The immediate

Admiral Cockburn looting Havre de Grace. *Anne S.K. Brown Military Collection, Brown University Library.*

effect, however, was that the Alexandria militia (then part of the District of Columbia militia) was quickly activated.

Earlier, the U.S. War Department had reorganized the District militia into two brigades. The Second Brigade consisted of an infantry regiment of Alexandria companies, including the privately outfitted Alexandria Blues, and a cavalry regiment composed of units from three jurisdictions: Alexandria (the Alexandria Dragoons), Washington and Georgetown. President Madison had appointed Alexandria merchant, shipowner and former council member Robert Young to lead this Second Brigade as a brigadier general.

In addition, Alexandrians over the age of forty-five, some of whom were veterans of the Revolutionary War, were moved by the "wanton destruction of Havre de Grace" to form the Company of Silver Grays to help defend the town.

In the days following the Havre-de-Grace incident, the militia units began to train seriously. Two months later, their training was put to some use when, on July 15, General Young learned that the British navy had entered the Potomac and was proceeding upriver. He immediately ordered his brigade under arms and into camp just south of town. The *Gazette* defiantly proclaimed: "Let them [the British navy] come here when they may, they will meet with a reception not very courteous."

However, after raiding farms and settlements in the lower part of the Potomac, the British ships were stopped from proceeding farther by the Kettle Bottoms, numerous shifting shoals of mud, sand and oyster shells roughly ninety miles downriver from Alexandria. By July 29, they were reported leaving the Potomac, and by the beginning of September 1813, most of the British ships had left the Chesapeake Bay.

Alexandrians could breathe easier. The British blockade had been relaxed, and the threat of attack on Alexandria had receded. The Alexandria militia, however, had not been tested. That soon would change.

Alexandrians vs. British Raiders, June 1814

At five thirty on the evening of Tuesday, June 21, 1814, a number of Alexandria cavalrymen were sitting on their horses on a hill overlooking the village of Benedict, Maryland, on the Patuxent River, about forty miles southeast of Washington. Below them, they could see several British barges and ships anchored in the river near the village.

Most of the British navy had departed the Chesapeake Bay in September the year before, leaving only a skeleton blockading squadron. However, in late February 1814, the British returned to the bay in force and resumed the pattern of shore raids they had pursued the previous year. Then Napoleon's defeat freed even more men and ships to fight in the Chesapeake.

Thus, this June evening, part of the British fleet had sailed up the Patuxent River to strike fear into the inhabitants there and to explore the river for possible future operations.

Two days earlier, a courier had ridden into Washington with the urgent message that the British were in the Patuxent River and had "burnt many dwellings and plundered a number of families" on the river's shores. In response, a force of District of Columbia militia—infantry, artillery and the cavalrymen from Alexandria, then part of the District—were assembled quickly in Washington and began marching toward the river.

The cavalry had ridden out ahead of the other units and were the first to reach the hills overlooking Benedict, where they found the British. The cavalrymen were citizen soldiers. The Alexandrians were led by Captain William F. Thornton, who normally would have been in Alexandria behind his druggist counter. With him on the hill was Alexander Hunter, twenty-four years old, whose store on King Street sold groceries, spirits and gunpowder. Also mounted on his horse on the hill was Francis Wise, the twenty-seven-year-old-son of John Wise, the owner of the hostelry today called Gadsby's Tavern. Although they did not know it, one of them was about to become the first Alexandria militiaman killed in the War of 1812.

On the hills above Benedict, they joined a small group of Maryland militia led by General Phillip Stuart, who also had been seeking the British. Two accounts of what happened next have survived. One was printed in Washington's *Daily National Intelligencer*, and the other appeared in the *Alexandria Gazette*.

Looking down from their hill, the cavalrymen saw in the distance the British vessels near the village. Closer, at the foot of their hill, they spotted "a small detachment of the enemy, probably a marauding party." Immediately, the order was given to charge. The troopers obeyed with "much haste and impetuosity."

Dashing down the hill and onto level ground, the cavalrymen quickly overtook three or four British soldiers on foot and took them prisoner. Continuing, the galloping horsemen pursued a group of several soldiers and a sergeant into an adjoining field. There, after a brief fight, they captured two or three of the soldiers and killed another, but the sergeant got away. A few cavalrymen went after him.

The *Gazette* version continues:

> Among the first who overtook him was Mr. Francis Wise of the Alexandria Dragoons who made a bold but unsuccessful assault upon him. Being unable to check his horse, [Wise] passed ten or fifteen paces beyond him. On turning his horse, Wise received the fire of the sergeant and fell dead. At this moment Mr. Alexander Hunter, a young gentleman of this town came up.

As the sergeant turned and faced Hunter, Hunter fired at him with his pistol, "which seemed to take effect." Then:

> Mr. Hunter's horse being alarmed at the [pistol's] report ran some distance from the spot. When Mr. H. returned, he found Gen. Stuart engaged with this intrepid soldier. He immediately advanced to the general's relief—upon which the sergeant having had his bayonet unshipped [disengaged from his musket], dropped his musket and mounting an adjoining fence fell upon the other side on his back.

His escape appearing certain unless pursued., Mr. H. begged the loan of a sword which was presented to him by the general, and with which he alone pursued and soon overtook [the sergeant]....A conflict ensued between them, the brave enemy endeavoring by many and vigorous efforts to get possession of the sword and refusing—though repeatedly urged,—to surrender except with his life.

Soon, his life, in fact, was ended with a stroke of Hunter's sword.

Meanwhile, the remainder of the marauding party had run back to their barges and ships in the river. The British vessels immediately opened up "a very brisk fire of round and grape shot" on the exposed Americans. General Stuart, seeing that the remainder of the British party had reached safety, ordered the Americans to retreat to the hills. They did so—amazingly, without further injury.

The British soldiers taken prisoner told the Americans that the slain sergeant was Sergeant Major Mayeaux or Mayo of the Royal Marines, with seventeen years of active service and a man "of great personal prowess." He, Trooper Wise and the British soldier slain earlier were buried "with the honors of war, by the Alexandria troop" near where they were killed. Their burial place is marked at Oldfields Episcopal Church near Hughesville, Maryland.

Two weeks later, the citizens of Georgetown gave the returning soldiers a rousing, celebratory dinner with a suitable number of toasts. The celebration, however, turned out to be premature.

The British and Enslaved People, July 1814

On July 23, 1814, Alexandrians read in the *Alexandria Gazette* that British ships again were sailing up the Potomac River and, further, that they had attacked the county seat of Calvert County, Maryland. The paper also reported news, disturbing to many Alexandrians, that when leaving the county seat, the British "carried off about 300 Slaves."

This news disturbed Alexandrians because, like their neighbors further down the Potomac, many owned Black enslaved people. In the 1810 census, 20 percent of Alexandria's population was enslaved. Although the *Gazette* articles suggested only that the British would take away enslaved Black Virginians as they would take away any property, Alexandrians knew, too,

Royal Colonial Marines. *Don Troiani.*

that the enslaved were perfectly capable of running away to the British on their own. The *Gazette* also reported that the British navy had been ordered "to receive and protect" escaped slaves and treat them as "free persons."

As a result, as historian Alan Taylor wrote, "The number of escapes surged during the summer and fall [of 1813] as word spread that the British officers welcomed runaways."

The first escapees to reach British ships sailing the Bay were young men. At times, whole families—men, women, and children—came together. They came to the British ships in stolen boats or canoes or met the British when they came ashore looking for water or for enslaved people to carry away.

The enslaved Virginians were well acquainted with the waters of the Chesapeake and the surrounding land. For years, they had been used in the bay as watermen in small boats, fishing, catching crabs, tonging oysters and transporting goods. On land, what little free time they had was mostly at night. While their masters slept, they would roam the woods and fields to hunt for meat, fish for themselves, meet future spouses, steal food, worship and dance. They became experts in the paths and byways of the land and the inlets of the bay and rivers. This knowledge not only helped them to escape but also, as the British gradually learned, helped them lead British raiding parties to farms and villages and then back to ships before the arrival of American militia.

When the British returned to the Chesapeake in force in early 1814, they enlisted Black male escapees into a British fighting force called the Colonial Marines. The marines were issued uniforms that included the British red coat and were trained at a fort established on Tangier Island in the Chesapeake Bay. The freed enslaved men were particularly valuable as soldiers, not only because they were considerably less likely to desert than White British sailors but also because they fed Whites' fear of Black ex-slaves armed and coming after them.

On August 13, Alexandrians learned that these armed Colonial Marines were on the lower Potomac. That day, the *Alexandria Gazette* reported that the British had landed at Monday's Point on the Yeocomico River on Virginia's Northern Neck. The British troops included "5 or 6 black platoons in red, commanded by British officers." They attacked Kinsale, burning houses and carrying away property. Outraged, the *Gazette* added, "Weep, Britain weep, and blush at the destitution and shame, which marks thy countrymen!"

On August 16, the *Gazette* reported that the British had left the Potomac. Alexandrians realized, however, that the British had come to the river in greater strength, with unexpected help, and might do so again.

ALEXANDRIA PREPARES ITS DEFENSE, AUGUST 1814

On August 20, 1814, General Robert Young, Alexandria merchant and commander of the Second Brigade of the District of Columbia Militia, received orders from his commander in Washington. His brigade, which contained all of Alexandria's infantry units, was to cross the Potomac River to Maryland, and there await further orders.

Disturbing news had reached Washington—the British navy in the Chesapeake Bay had been heavily reinforced. To many in Washington, this clearly meant that the British were preparing a major attack, and they were its target. In anticipation, federal government authorities, whose main concern was protecting the capital, not Alexandria, decided that the best place for Young and his brigade was Maryland.

Alexandria's militiamen were under federal control, and they had been sent away from Alexandria. If its own soldiers were not available to protect against a British attack, what other resources did the town have?

That question had concerned Alexandrians for some time. A year and a half earlier, in February 1813, Mayor Charles Simms wrote Secretary of War John Armstrong about the town's inability to defend against "any predatory attempt that may possibly be made against it from the enemy fleet." He continued, "It would be very practicable to land three or four hundred men in the night who might plunder the Banks, Stores, dwelling houses and Shipping without resistance and make good their retreat before effectual steps could be taken to prevent it."

Mayor Simms, then fifty-nine years old, was a veteran of the Revolutionary War. He had served as a colonel under George Washington, who had written of him, "He is a brave intelligent and good Officer." After that war, Simms and his wife had moved to Alexandria, where he had become a successful attorney, occasionally representing George Washington. Simms had been elected mayor a year earlier, and he would lead Alexandria throughout the War of 1812. Naturally, he was concerned about the town's safety.

Colo. Charles Simms, Gentleman
(Drawn by Mrs. J. O. Estabrook from Miniature)

Alexandria mayor Colonel Charles Simms. *Internet Archive.*

Apparently, there was no favorable response to his letter, and the Alexandria Common

Council decided to do what it could in its own defense. On May 8, 1813, it appropriated $1,500 for mounting the town's guns, including two twelve-pound cannons at Jones Point, and paying expenses already incurred in mounting "two brass field pieces," both six-pounders. (The use of "pound" in connection with cannons refers to the weight of the ball the cannon fired.)

That same day, the council also decided to go to the top with its plea for federal aid. It appointed a committee, headed by Mayor Simms, to meet with President Madison. The meeting took place several days later, and Simms summarized its results: "He [President Madison] observed, that the representation of any respectable body of men was entitled to attention; and that the subject should be taken under consideration, or words to that effect."

The president delivered this brushoff despite Simms having known Madison since 1776, when Madison and Simms had both been delegates to Virginia's first constitutional convention. Simms had represented the frontier town of Fort Dunmore (later known as Pittsburgh, but in 1776 considered part of Virginia), and Madison had represented Orange County. In 1813, however, Simms and Madison were in opposing political parties, a fact that probably did not help Alexandria's cause.

Also, in May 1813, a few days after the meeting with the president, deputations from Alexandria, Washington and Georgetown met with Secretary of War Armstrong, urging him to increase the District's defenses. They urged him particularly to strengthen Fort Washington (also known then as Fort Warburton), located about six miles downriver from Alexandria, the last line of defense against enemy ships sailing up the Potomac River to Washington or Alexandria.

The fort itself was situated on a level area of less than four acres much lower and nearer the water than the Fort Washington existing today. Major Pierre L'Enfant, military engineer and architect of the capital city, was sent in May 1813 to examine the fort. He reported that it and its weapons were in a dilapidated condition, adding that "the whole original design was bad, and it is therefore impossible to make a perfect work of it by any alterations."

Two months later, a General Wilkinson examined the fort. His July report also criticized its design, saying the fort was a "mere water battery" whose cannons could not be swiveled to shoot at ships once they had gotten past them. Also, on the bluff above the fort was a two-story brick blockhouse that "could be knocked down by a twelve-pounder [cannon]." Many British warships then carried twenty-four-pound cannons or larger.

But little or nothing was done to correct these deficiencies. A year later, in July 1814, the overall military commander of the District, General William H. Winder, wrote, "Fort Washington is, in several respects, incomplete in its state of preparation for defense."

Finally, some ammunition was sent to the fort along with two men to make repairs, but these measures were sadly inadequate.

On August 18, two days before Alexandria's militia was ordered out of town, the *Alexandria Gazette* announced that banks in Georgetown, Washington and Alexandria had agreed to loan the federal government $200,000, half to be used for "the erection of permanent fortifications upon the shores of the Potomac." Three banks in Alexandria soon provided $50,000 toward this goal.

As it turned out, however, there was no time left to spend the money as intended. Mayor Simms and Alexandria were left with no militia, a fort incompletely prepared and a few small cannons.

Battle of Bladensburg, August 1814

On August 18, 1814, authorities in Washington learned that British warships were sailing up the Patuxent River in considerable force. Was Washington their target? Taking no chances, the authorities immediately ordered the District of Columbia militiamen, including the Alexandria Brigade under General Robert Young, to report for duty.

Simultaneously, they ordered General Young to dispatch the Alexandria Dragoons to meet Secretary of State James Monroe in Maryland at four o'clock the next morning. Several days later, the dragoons would ride with Monroe to the fiasco of the Battle of Bladensburg, the British victory that enabled the British army to seize Washington.

More immediately, Monroe had volunteered to ride to the Patuxent "to find and reconnoiter the enemy." No one seemed to think it unusual for a fifty-six-year-old secretary of state to go on a scouting expedition, but Monroe was a veteran of the Revolutionary War with a bullet wound in his shoulder to prove it. Thus, on August 19 at one o'clock in the afternoon, Monroe rode out to seek the British accompanied by twenty-five or thirty Alexandria dragoons as his escorts and messengers.

The dragoons were led, as they had been on their adventurous ride to the Patuxent in June, by Alexandria druggist Captain William H. Thornton.

Secretary of State James Monroe and the Alexandria Dragoons scout British soldiers landing at Benedict, Maryland. *National Park Service/© Gerry Embleton.*

Members of the dragoons included relatives of several prominent Alexandrians. Young privates Thomas and William Herbert were sons of Thomas Herbert, president of the Common Council. Cornet Samuel Thompson, twenty-one, was the son of prosperous merchant and wharf owner Jonah Thompson of 209–211 North Fairfax Street, for whom Thompson's Alley is named. Private Robert Conway, age twenty-two, was the nephew of former mayor Richard Conway, who in 1789 had loaned money to George Washington so Washington could clear his Virginia debts and go to New York to become president of the United States.

On the morning of the twentieth, Monroe and the Alexandria Dragoons arrived on a hill overlooking the Patuxent about three miles from Benedict, Maryland. Monroe quickly sent one of the dragoons to President Madison with the news that the British were disembarking numerous soldiers

at Benedict. Where they were headed—to Washington, Annapolis or Baltimore—was unclear.

For the next several days, Monroe continued to follow the British army as it marched north generally parallel to the Patuxent River, and he continued to send, by the fast-riding dragoons, messages about the enemy's movements and strength to General William H. Winder, the American army's commander, President Madison, and even the French ambassador.

Although General Winder commanded the American army, he had only limited military experience, and that experience included blundering into the British lines near Lake Ontario, being captured and remaining a prisoner for almost a year. While the British army was marching through Maryland, the American army under Winder only monitored the British from afar while repeatedly moving backward and forward, uncertain as to the enemy's destination. Historian Henry Adams wrote, "Thus for five full days a British army marched in a leisurely manner through a long-settled country and met no show of resistance."

Finally, it was clear that the British were marching toward Washington by way of Bladensburg, a town of about 1,500 inhabitants on the east bank of the Eastern Branch (now the Anacostia River) six miles from Washington. There, the road to Washington led over a bridge crossing the branch at a spot where it narrowed and could be waded easily.

On the morning of August 24, Winder ordered his army to Bladensburg. There, the army was positioned disjointedly by individual unit commanders; by Monroe, employing Captain Thornton's Alexandria Dragoons; and by Winder into three parallel lines on the west side of the branch facing the British in the town on the opposite bank. The lines, however, were too far apart to support each other effectively.

Early in the afternoon, the British charged. After being checked briefly by fire from the Americans, these veterans of battles against Napoleon quickly rallied, crossed the bridge or waded through the branch and swept through the Americans' three lines one at a time, driving most of the largely inexperienced and tired American soldiers off to Washington at a run.

President Madison, Secretary of State Monroe and other civil leaders were near the first line when the battle started. They soon moved to a place behind the third line, and when all appeared lost, they hastily retreated into Washington and then through it to the Virginia or Maryland countryside.

The Alexandria Dragoons also retreated, but it is unclear what they did next. Some probably accompanied Monroe as he moved about the Maryland countryside, but many of them had been dispersed earlier in various directions while carrying messages. As a captain of another American cavalry unit reported: "The Alexandria troop…had so many detached on duties [elsewhere], as left but a few scattering ones on the field [at Bladensburg]."

In the meantime, Alexandria's infantry under General Young missed the Bladensburg battle entirely. Initially, it had been assigned a position in Maryland three miles behind Fort Washington to guard the fort from attack by land. Then, on the morning of the battle, Young was ordered to abandon that position and march to the Eastern Branch bridge into Washington. Before he reached that new position, however, he was ordered to cross the Potomac into Virginia. Then, after some of his men had embarked on boats to take them across the river, he received new orders to occupy a position north of Fort Washington. Finally, as the main army was retreating through Washington, Young again received orders to cross to Virginia, which he wearily did that night. Encamped west of Alexandria, he awaited further orders.

Meanwhile, word reached Washington and Alexandria that seven British warships were sailing up the Potomac River with only the poorly designed Fort Washington blocking their way.

ALEXANDRIA SURRENDERS, AUGUST 1814

On August 24, 1814, the day of the Battle of Bladensburg, Alexandria mayor Charles Simms called an urgent meeting of Alexandria's Common Council, the town's governing body, to discuss what to do as the British approached Alexandria by land and by water. As they met, worried Alexandrians in homes all around town debated whether to stay or flee.

Council members knew the British army was approaching Washington by way of Bladensburg and the British navy was some thirty miles below Alexandria, sailing up the Potomac River. They also surely remembered that in a similar situation the previous year, the British navy destroyed Havre de Grace, Maryland, and that only a month ago, the British were on the lower Potomac burning buildings and welcoming the area's enslaved people aboard their ships.

They also knew that General William Winder, the commander of the District of Columbia land forces, had ordered the Alexandria militia out of Alexandria, along with all the town's cannons, except for two lacking ammunition. Earlier that day, the council had sent a deputation to General Winder to determine how he planned to defend Alexandria. His response was not encouraging.

Without militiamen, with only two useless cannons and without help from the federal government, the council realized it had no defense against the British army should it come to Alexandria, and the only thing that lay between Alexandria and the British navy was Fort Washington. Thus, the council passed a resolution:

> *That, in case the British vessels should pass the fort, or their forces approach the town by land, and there should be no sufficient force on our part to oppose them with any reasonable prospect of success, they* [the Council] *should appoint a committee to carry a flag* [of truce] *to the officer commanding the enemy's force about to attack the town, and to procure the best terms for the safety of persons, houses, and property, in their power.*

Events moved faster than the council had anticipated. By the end of the day they met, the British army had defeated the Americans at Bladensburg and was in Washington burning buildings. General Winder and the American army had retreated well west of the city. President Madison and his cabinet were scattered throughout the countryside. The Alexandria militia's position was unknown.

The next morning, August 25, a delegation of four Alexandrians appointed by the council crossed the river and found one of the two commanders of the British forces, Rear Admiral George Cockburn, at his headquarters across from the smoldering Capitol. The four men were Rev. Dr. James Muir, minister of the congregation known today as the Old Presbyterian Meeting House; Dr. Elisha Cullen Dick, a medical doctor who had attended George Washington in his last illness; Jonathan Swift, a prominent merchant; and William Swann, a young lawyer.

Unsure of the army's next move, they asked Admiral Cockburn, who had destroyed Havre de Grace, what treatment their town might expect if the army captured it. His reply: "[A]ll I have to say is that we want provisions… but…for every article we take, you shall be allowed a fair price." Considering this response the best they would get, the delegation returned to Alexandria.

Meanwhile, Georgetowners had been trying to surrender to the British for two days. Not finding anyone on the twenty-fourth, they located Major General Robert Ross, the British army commander, on the twenty-fifth and offered to hand over their town if their houses were spared. Ross said he would think about it.

The following morning, the twenty-sixth, Alexandrians awoke to find that the British army had left Washington during the night. Its departure apparently nullified Cockburn's pronouncements. Now the town would have to wait for the British navy, steadily advancing upriver, and its confrontation with Fort Washington. Later that day, the council cautiously appointed a delegation of three—Mayor Simms, Jonathan Swift, and Edmund J. Lee, former council member and uncle of young Robert E. Lee—to approach the commander of the navy squadron with a surrender flag, if the squadron passed the fort.

They did not have long to wait. The next day, the twenty-seventh, the British were opposite Fort Washington. As the council later wrote: "The citizens [of Alexandria] looked with great anxiety to [the fort] for protection; but, to their great surprise and mortification…the fort was abandoned, and the magazine blown up by the United States' garrison on the evening of the 27th, without firing a single gun."

The following morning, Alexandrians standing on their waterfront wharves saw smoke rising in the north from the remains of the Capitol burned by the British and, to the south, British ships. By ten o'clock, according to a report of the council, part of the British squadron had passed the fort. The council met again and passed a resolution saying, "The Common Council has considered itself authorized from extreme necessity" to make an arrangement with the enemy to ensure the town's safety.

The committee appointed earlier took a small boat to meet the British squadron's commander, Captain James Gordon, on his flagship *Seahorse* to learn his surrender terms. Gordon was only thirty-one, but he had served as a captain under British naval hero Lord Nelson and wore a wooden leg to replace one lost to a French cannonball. Gordon said that when he arrived at Alexandria, he would let them know.

The next morning, Alexandrians found seven warships with a total of over one hundred cannons plus mortars and rockets approaching the town or moored "but a few hundred yards from the wharves, and the houses so situated that they might have been laid in ashes in a few minutes," according to the council's report.

That morning, Captain Gordon sent Mayor Simms his terms. He would neither destroy the town nor molest its inhabitants if the Alexandrians would not fight and would surrender all naval stores, shipping in the

British ships in Alexandria's harbor. *Patrick O'Brien/Hal Hardaway.*

harbor and merchandise in town intended for export. He gave the town one hour to reply.

The council, having no other choice, agreed.

The British promptly began removing ships from Alexandria's wharves and tobacco, cotton, flour, wine and other commodities from the town's warehouses.

ALEXANDRIA LOOTED, AUGUST AND SEPTEMBER 1814

On August 29, 1814, Alexandrians had seven warships of the British navy anchored opposite their waterfront with numerous cannons aimed at their town, and they surrendered.

That afternoon, the British, helped by enslaved men, began emptying the warehouses lining Alexandria's harbor of flour, tobacco, cotton, rice, wine and other goods. They placed the goods in ships' boats and rowed them out to the warships or loaded them onto captured American vessels in the harbor to take with them later as prizes. Alexandria merchants stood by, "viewing with melancholy countenance the British sailors gutting their warehouses of their contents," a newspaperman reported.

John Lloyd, a successful merchant and future owner of the Lloyd House and Lloyd's Row on Washington Street, probably was one of these merchants. Later, he swore under oath that the British "forcibly took from his possession in Alexandria three hundred and fifty-two barrels of superfine flour."

Many Alexandrians, however, had left or were sent from town to avoid the British. The frightened parents of seven-year-old Matilda Roberts bundled her into a four-horse wagon, her precious tea set sitting in her lap, to be driven to a location ten miles out of town. Very likely also leaving Alexandria to stay with relatives in the Virginia countryside were seven-year-old Robert E. Lee and his mother, two brothers and two sisters. A visitor to Alexandria at this time found the town "almost deserted."

Other people also were leaving the Alexandria area, but for a different reason. At midnight on the first night that the British ships were anchored off Alexandria, twenty-four enslaved people, at least some of them owned by Alexandrians, escaped and boarded one of those ships.

The movement of people, however, was not all one way. At least two British sailors deserted from British ships in Alexandria.

The British did keep their agreement not to molest Alexandrians. Mayor Charles Simms, the fifty-nine-year-old Revolutionary War veteran, remained in town. He wrote to his wife, Nancy, who had left Alexandria with their children, "It is impossible that men could behave better than the British behaved while the town was in their power, not a single inhabitant was insulted or injured by them in their persons or homes."

All did not go entirely smoothly, however, because of the actions of three American naval officers, Captain David Porter, Captain John Creighton and Lieutenant Charles Platt.

Captain Porter had just returned to the United States from the Pacific Ocean, where he had harassed British whaling ships and fought a valiant battle against a superior British naval force in the harbor of Valparaiso, Chile. When he arrived in Philadelphia in July, he was given a hero's welcome. Just outside the city, Philadelphians even removed the horses from his carriage, substituted themselves and pulled the carriage and the triumphant Porter into the city. The secretary of the navy then ordered Porter to report to Washington to help defend it against the British. He arrived too late to save the Capitol, however, and was ordered to Alexandria to help develop a plan to stop the British navy.

Unlike Porter, Captain Creighton had been in Washington only a week earlier as the British approached the city. Then he had helped burn the Washington Navy Yard to keep it from falling into British hands. Destroyed in the fire was the ship Creighton was to command.

On September 1, both officers plus Lieutenant Platt were on Shuters Hill in Alexandria.

What appears to have happened that day (accounts differ) is that the three officers donned civilian clothes and rode their horses into Alexandria. They stopped first at the Washington Tavern on King Street with the sign showing George Washington on horseback mounted over the door. Finding no Englishmen there, they rode on down King to Union Street.

Once there, they looked to their right and saw British midshipman John Fraser, no older than his early teens, "sauntering leisurely" back to a ship's barge tied to the wharf at the foot of Prince Street. Either Porter or Creighton (again, accounts differ) immediately spurred his horse down Union Street, grabbed the midshipman by a handkerchief tied around his neck and began pulling him onto his horse's back. "The youngster, quite astonished, kicked and squalled most lustily," relates one account. The attempted abduction failed, however, when the midshipman's neckerchief came untied and the midshipman fell to the ground.

Captain David Porter seizes a British midshipman. *National Park Service/© Gerry Embleton.*

The Americans then rode rapidly down Union Street, up Duke and out of town while the midshipman ran to the barge. He scrambled aboard, and the seamen rowed him quickly back to their ship.

British captain Gordon was informed of what had happened. Immediately, he ordered the warships' portholes opened and cannons run out. Throughout the town, women and children fled "screaming through the streets," Mayor Sims later wrote.

Simms, however, acted quickly. He informed Gordon the town lacked control over the three naval officers, and the crisis was averted.

Earlier that same day, orders reached Captain Gordon to return to the fleet, and he ordered his warships to begin sailing back downriver with the prize ships.

Meanwhile, the Americans had developed a plan that would ensure Gordon's passage downriver would be unpleasant, and for a change, the Alexandria militia finally would fight the British.

NEW BATTLE PLAN, AUGUST 1814

On August 31, 1814, General John Hungerford, a congressman from the Northern Neck in command of about two thousand militiamen from several Virginia counties, was encamped with his men on Shuter's Hill, where the Masonic Memorial stands today. For days earlier, they had been monitoring Gordon's ships as they sailed up the Potomac. However, Hungerford had fallen behind and arrived at Alexandria after the ships.

Earlier, as Hungerford approached Alexandria, the Alexandria Common Council had urged him not to enter the town and risk the peace the council had negotiated with the British. Acting Secretary of War James Monroe had concurred and ordered Hungerford to camp to the west of the town.

Thus, for two days from atop the hill, Hungerford and his men watched the British squadron in the Alexandria harbor "lying in full view below us...with all hands engaged in loading the vessels found at the wharf...with tobacco and flour," one of the militiamen wrote.

On the thirty-first, Hungerford was joined on Shuter's Hill by Monroe; Captain David Porter, the thirty-four-year-old hero of American naval actions in the Pacific; and possibly Secretary of the Navy William Jones. They developed a plan to harass the British ships as they voyaged back down the Potomac.

Part of the plan was for Captain Porter to lead an American force about twelve miles below Alexandria to Belvoir Neck, the peninsula just south of Mount Vernon, the present home of Fort Belvoir. There, Porter would erect batteries of cannons and position militiamen "to endeavor to effect the destruction of the Enemy's Squadron on its passage down the Potomac."

Porter's force was to consist of about one hundred seamen he had brought with him, General Hungerford and his men and General Robert Young and his brigade of Alexandrians.

After crossing from Maryland through Alexandria to the northern Virginia countryside on the night of August 24, General Young and his brigade of about 450 Alexandrians had investigated a report that a slave rebellion was being organized in northern Virginia, a report that turned out to be false. They then had crossed the Potomac again into Maryland and proceeded to the President's House, as the White House then was called. From their location near the burned shell of the President's House, they were poised to defend Washington should the British navy advance there from Alexandria. As Young reported, they were "in full view of the enemy's fleet" lying in his hometown of Alexandria. They had yet to fire a shot at that enemy.

Captain David Porter, James Monroe and others atop Alexandria's Shuter's Hill plan an attack. *National Park Service/© Gerry Embleton.*

As General Young recorded later, his brigade consisted of "persons from all situations in life." It included young Private William Herbert Jr., grandson of the president of the Bank of Alexandria; Private Samuel Baggett, a twenty-five-year-old laborer; and fifty-two-year-old Drummer Domini Barcroff, a free Black man, owner of a popular Alexandria tavern on Fairfax Street.

It also included twenty-seven-year-old Captain Greenberry Griffith, commander of the Alexandria artillery and an Alexandria silversmith. He had with him Alexandria's two six-pound cannons and one four-pound cannon. He also had the town's two twelve-pound cannons that Young had taken with him the night of the twenty-fourth as the brigade marched through Alexandria on its way west. Later, while the British were looting Alexandria, Griffith's men retrieved powder from the Alexandria powder house and sponges, rammers and other items necessary to work the guns from the gun house. At Belvoir Neck, Griffith would obtain ammunition and play a leading role in the battle against the British ships.

On August 31, Young received his orders and ordered his men back across the Potomac to join Porter's force at Belvoir Neck. Young himself rode ahead the morning of September 1 to join Porter, Hungerford and their men for the march to Belvoir Neck. Before they left Shuter's Hill, Captain Porter rode into Alexandria with two other officers to reconnoiter and tried to kidnap the midshipman, as related earlier.

The banks of the Potomac at Belvoir Neck where the force was headed were some forty feet high and heavily wooded. There, the river channel ran close to the bank, meaning that sailing downriver, the British ships must move close to where the Americans were mounting their cannons. Lower and close to the river's edge stood a white-painted house known as the White House, a feature that gave its name to that area.

While marching toward the White House, Porter received word from militiamen sent ahead to fell trees to clear a place for the cannons that a British ship was approaching the White House. Accompanied by two four-pound cannons, Porter rode quickly on ahead.

When Porter, his cannons and cannoneers arrived at the edge of the bluff where Hungerford's militiamen had cleared away trees, they saw within a half mile a British brig floating unsuspectingly upriver toward them with the tide. "The few sails she had set were flapping as she rolled with the sullen swell, her rigging and yards were hung with shirts and trousers, it being washing day," a militiaman wrote years later. "Her deck was covered with men....She stood close in to the shore, not seeming to regard the few men she saw on the banks."

As the brig approached, the militiamen who had been felling trees lay down flat on the ground to hide. Porter fired a shot from each of the two cannons. One cannonball skipped across the water in front of the brig's bow, and the other cut down a signal flag that fell into the water. The men on deck, however, paid no attention, apparently thinking it was only a small party of neighborhood militia.

One of the cannons fired again, and this third shot struck the ship's hull. At the same time, the militiamen rose and fired their muskets at the men on deck. Immediately, the Americans heard men scream and saw the British sailors vanish belowdecks.

The brig then managed to fire a broadside, but the cannonballs struck the bank below the Americans. Meanwhile, the Americans continued to fire their muskets "until the shirts and trousers were cut into bits." As the brig moved away, Porter fired a last cannon shot that shattered the glass window at its stern.

This ship was the British armed brig *Fairy*. It was its cutter that, earlier, gave Captain Gordon in Alexandria the order to rejoin the fleet and let him know that his descent of the Potomac would be contested.

That night, Hungerford and Porter's men arrived at the White House. The next day, September 2, the men of Alexandria's brigade arrived also. They had yet to fire a shot at the British or be fired on by the British. That would change before the day was over.

ALEXANDRIA FIGHTS BACK, SEPTEMBER 1814

On September 2, 1814, General Robert Young and the infantry part of his brigade of Alexandrians arrived on Belvoir Neck, twelve miles south of Alexandria, at an area called White House Landing. The Alexandria artillery, which moved slower, would arrive the next day.

There, on the edge of a forty-foot-high bluff overlooking the river, the Americans under the overall command of navy captain David Porter had established a battery of cannons protected by infantry, about two thousand men altogether. Their goal was to destroy the British warships as they sailed back down the Potomac River from Alexandria.

On the other hand, the British were determined to destroy the battery. The British sailed five ships, including two bomb ships and a rocket ship, into position to launch a bombardment. For three days, these warships fired their cannon balls, bombshells and rockets almost continuously, day and night.

The bomb ships carried squat four-ton mortars that fired shells that flew in a high arc and could be set to explode on the ground or in midair. The rocket ship fired Congreve rockets, projectiles about three-and-a-half feet long that soared up into the air like skyrockets, "hissing and roaring, trailing flame and smoke…and exploded with a thunderous clap, showering shards of metal," wrote historian Steve Vogel. (Later, in the harbor at Baltimore, these identical ships sent "bombs bursting in air" and produced "the rocket's red glare.")

When Young's Alexandrians arrived, they were assigned a position behind the American battery Porter had established. Here, they were available to protect the battery if the British launched a land attack. They still, however, were within range of the British weapons.

Among them was twenty-four-year-old Private Richard Cranch Norton. Norton, a great-nephew of Abigail and John Adams, recently had moved to Alexandria from Massachusetts to practice law. Norton later recorded in his journal that "until [the battle], I never knew what it was to hear the whistling of cannon balls, shells, etc. At first it was not very agreeable music to a new soldier like myself, but custom soon makes everything familiar to us."

On the third, Captain Greenberry Griffith, the twenty-seven-year-old Alexandria silversmith, arrived in camp with his Alexandria artillery and its six- and twelve-pound cannons. Porter immediately ordered him into action beside the battery already in place, bringing the number of effective cannons on the bluff to thirteen.

The next day, September 4, the British rocket ship moved closer to shore. In response, Captain Porter ordered some of his sailors, with a twelve-pound cannon, and Griffith, with Alexandria's two six-pounders, to a point close to the ship.

Porter later reported that the enemy rocket ship "was much cut up" by the American cannons.

> Scarcely a shot missed his hull, and for one hour we drew to this point, the fire of all the enemy's force.…The intrepidity of Captain Griffith of the Alexandria Artillery, his officers and men, merit the highest eulogiums.… They fought their six-pounders until their ammunition was expended and coolly retired with their guns when ordered to do so under a shower of the enemy's shot.

The rocket ship soon pulled back to repair damage to sails and rigging and to commit to the depths of the Potomac two of its seamen killed in the action as its wounded captain looked on.

Later, Captain Charles Napier, captain of the HMS *Euryalus*, complained that the Americans had loaded their cannons with "every sort of devilment," such as "nails, broken pokers, gun barrels—everything that will do mischief." He groused, "A 24-lb shot in the stomach is fine—we die heroically; but a brass candlestick for stuffing, with a garnish of rusty two penny nails, makes us die ungenteely."

That same day, the first Alexandrian was killed. He was a small, "very sprightly" boy. The boy's mother, a widow in Alexandria, had allowed him to accompany an officer "who had greatly befriended her." The boy was running after a spent cannon ball when another ball flew through the air, struck him and killed him.

On September 5, all eight of the British warships and the twenty-one captured merchant vessels loaded with Alexandria's goods were assembled

Weapons used in the White House Landing Battle. *National Park Service/© Gerry Embleton.*

for an attempt to pass the battery. Around noon, led by two frigates—HMS *Seahorse*, with thirty-eight guns, and HMS *Euryalus*, with thirty-six—they got under way. The frigates had cut away the upper parts of their portholes to elevate their cannons sufficiently to fire effectively on the battery on the high bluff. They anchored close to the shore and began to fire their cannons continuously with round and grapeshot.

The other warships and prizes followed them. Captain Porter later reported that all the British warships were "pouring into the battery and neighboring woods a tremendous fire of every description of missiles."

General Young had detached some of his Alexandrians to join a unit from Essex County, Virginia, positioned to the right of the battery. From there, they and the other militiamen poured "well-directed fire on the Enemy's deck," Porter later wrote.

Alexandrians now were in the middle of the enemy bombardment. Cannonballs from the ships screamed overhead. "The crashing in the woods with which the shore in this place is covered, was prodigious," Private Norton later recorded. "Large trees were cut down in numerous instances…and the limbs and splinters fell in every direction." Nearby, gunnery officers yelled "Fire," American cannons crashed and muskets cracked. Powder smoke drifted among the Alexandria men and into their eyes. Sweat streamed down their faces.

Finally, the barrage from the eight British ships became so destructive that most of the outgunned American cannons were disabled. (A broadside from just one British frigate was eighteen cannons. The Americans' cannons totaled only thirteen.) Porter ordered a retreat, and the British ships ceased firing. By 2:50 p.m., almost three hours after their bombardment began, all British ships had passed the battery.

The British had seven killed and thirty-five wounded. The Americans lost eleven killed and seventeen or eighteen wounded. Two Alexandrians were listed as killed in the battle. One was Private Robert Allison Jr., who served in the Alexandria artillery. A Samuel Bowen also was listed, but it is unclear whether he was a soldier or the unnamed Alexandria boy killed by the cannonball.

The Alexandrians and all the militiamen had performed well—much better than the militia at Bladensburg. Captain Porter wrote that they "conducted themselves in a manner which reflects on them and their Country the highest honor."

Although the Americans had not sunk a single British ship, they had delayed the rendezvous of Gordon's squadron, particularly its bomb and rocket ships, with the rest of the British fleet. Thus, the fleet's attack on Baltimore was delayed, and Baltimore had additional time to strengthen its defenses, defeat the British and continue to fly the Star-Spangled Banner.

THE WAR OF 1812—WHO WON?

After the British left Washington, Alexandria and the Potomac River, their luck changed. On September 12–14, 1814, the Americans defeated them at Baltimore and on January 8, 1815, defeated them again at New Orleans.

Even before the Battle of New Orleans, the British had had enough of war. They and the American negotiators signed a treaty to end the war in Ghent, Belgium, on December 24, 1814. The United States Senate ratified it, and President Madison signed it on February 16, 1815. The War of 1812 finally was over.

Who won the war—the British or the Americans—or was it a draw? What about Alexandria?

Before the British left the Potomac River, the District of Columbia's brigade of Alexandrians at White House Landing had helped retrieve some honor for the Americans after the disgraceful Battle of Bladensburg. Many Americans, however, focused on Alexandria's surrender to the British navy, not its valiant fight against the British as they sailed down the Potomac.

The criticism began even before the British left Alexandria. On September 1, Washington's *National Intelligencer* wrote, somewhat inaccurately: "The degrading terms dictated by the Commander of the British squadron below Alexandria…connected with the offer of the townsmen *before* the squadron had even reached the fort, to surrender without resistance…have everywhere excited *astonishment and indignation.*" The *Richmond Enquirer* wrote on August 31, "Thanks be to the Almighty God: that this degraded town no longer forms part of the state of *Virginia.*"

The editor of the *Alexandria Gazette*, Samuel Snowden, countered by setting out Alexandria's numerous efforts to get the federal government to help with its defense. The government, however, not only provided no help but also ordered away the town's soldiers. Snowden proclaimed that under these circumstances, to call Alexandrians cowardly was "matchless impudence! Unparalleled libel upon the character of a virtuous and high-minded people."

Gradually, however, the rehabilitation of Alexandria's image began. Congress had appointed a committee to inquire into the invasion of

Washington and Alexandria. The committee issued its report on November 29, 1814, and it included detailed statements submitted by the Alexandria Common Council and others, setting forth the circumstances leading to the surrender. Although the committee report contained no conclusion, it was clear that Alexandria was defenseless and had no choice but to surrender.

On December 11, 1815, the city celebrated its contribution to the Battle of White House Landing with an "elegant dinner" at what today is Gadsby's Tavern, complete with a band, firing of cannons and thirty grand toasts.

Alexandria's defense may have been expressed most forcefully years later by Major John S. Williams, who had served in the District of Columbia militia during the war. In 1857, he wrote:

> *There was no possible means of defense or resistance; for even if the old men, women, and children, who were left in the town, had wrought themselves up to the pitch of desperate valor...and resorted to pitchforks, pokers, tongs, and brick-bats, all these would have availed nothing against a bombardment by a naval force.*

As for the war's impact on the United States generally, the treaty itself did not change the relationship between Britain and the United States on issues that caused the war. It contained no language about preventing the British from seizing American ships or impressing American seamen. It also was silent about international trade restrictions. On the other hand, the British no longer were in a deadly war with France and did not need additional ships or additional seamen. In fact, they were mothballing ships and putting seamen on dry land, and Americans never again were subject to those practices.

When the war ended, the British still controlled Canada, but instead of heading north, Americans expanded into the vast continent to the west. In 1813, an American army unit had defeated the Shawnee leader Tecumseh, making westward expansion safer—an expansion that ultimately resolved another issue that had led to the war, Indian attacks.

Perhaps the Americans did not win the war in the traditional way, but at the war's end, they were better off than they were in the beginning. Perhaps the biggest change was the increase in the country's prestige and pride. The United States had won the last two major battles against the vaunted British army. Throughout the war, the American navy had embarrassed the storied British navy in ship-to-ship combat. The United States had the potential to become a great power on both land and sea.

Homes at 609 and 611 Cameron Street today that were built before 1814 and the British navy could have destroyed. Three-year-old Robert E. Lee lived in the house on the left when his family first moved to Alexandria in 1810. *Author's collection.*

These were things other nations noted, things to take pride in. The war also gave the United States new, powerful symbols, such as the flag that flew over Baltimore's Fort McHenry and the future national anthem, "The Star-Spangled Banner."

Also, to some extent, this war was a second War of Independence. Although Britain never seriously challenged America's independence, it did not seriously respect America's sovereignty, either. That began to change after the war. "I must acknowledge that the war has been useful," wrote Albert Gallatin. "The character of America stands now as high as ever on the European continent, and higher than ever it did in Great Britain." Never again did Britain and the United States go to war against each other.

Although the war did not go as the Americans hoped, the United States did come out of it in a better position than when they entered it. French ambassador Louis Serurier wrote to his superior Tallyrand: "Finally, the war has given the Americans what they so essentially lacked, a national character founded on glory common to all."

The War of 1812 and Alexandrians' actions during the war have largely faded from national memory. What has endured are the Alexandria buildings that might have been lost had the British ships aimed their 117 cannons at the town and fired. Fitzgerald Warehouse, Gadsby's Tavern, the Carlyle House and other homes and buildings remain among us. In fact, they are the essence of Alexandria.

Chapter 6

THE DARK DAYS
OF THE BLACK CODES

Fourteen-year-old Nancy Jones was scared. She had been stopped by a policeman while walking down a street in Washington, D.C., and he had asked to see her papers. Nancy had good cause to be afraid. She was an African American, and it was 1835. And she did not have the papers. The policeman immediately arrested her as a runaway slave. Yet Nancy was not enslaved and never had been.

Most of us know that there were enslaved and non-enslaved African Americans in the District of Columbia before the Civil War. In fact, slavery was not abolished in the District of Columbia until April 1862, a year after the Civil War began. In 1835, the year Nancy was arrested, the population of Washington was only about twenty-one thousand (not including Georgetown, then a separate city, and the parts of Virginia then in the District). A little more than a quarter of those were African American, roughly one-third enslaved and two-thirds free.

But even the non-enslaved, like Nancy, were not entirely free—if they were Black. Washington and the southern states had special laws governing African Americans, both enslaved and free, known as black codes. Under Washington's code in effect in 1835, a free Black person had to be home by ten o'clock in the evening and had to post a bond of $500 guaranteeing his or her good behavior. By laws inherited from Maryland and Virginia, a Black person could not testify against a White person, hold office or vote.

Probably the most severe provision of the code was the one that affected Nancy. Under the law, that she was in fact free made no difference. A Black

The Slave Market in Washington, D.C., detail of an 1836 poster. *Library of Congress.*

person without papers proving she (or he) was free was legally a runaway slave and could be jailed. If no White person got her out, she would be sold as a slave and the money received would go to pay her jail fees. According to some historians, any excess amount then went not to the city but into the pockets of the jailer and the district marshal.

It may be difficult for us today to comprehend how limited freedom was for a "free" Black person then, but an examination of Nancy's case in the old files of the U.S. Circuit Court for the D.C. Circuit and other documents of the time can help bring that period to life. Such an examination also demonstrates that, although we may not realize it, what we do in court today may be an element of history tomorrow.

In Nancy's case, the first item is her commitment order. It indicates that on May 4, 1835, she was brought before a magistrate by Constable John Stevenson. From other records in the file, we know that when she stood before the magistrate, she was only four feet, ten inches tall and wore a light calico dress. She told the authorities that her father was George Jones, a free Black man living in Baltimore. She said he lived in one of Mr. Mullinix's houses there and that Mullinix, a White man, knew she was not enslaved.

A young Black woman standing in front of an Alexandria slave jail circa 1862. *Library of Congress*.

The magistrate ignored her and sent her to jail.

The jail was an old two-story building on what is now Washington, D.C.'s Judiciary Square. As it was described in grand jury investigations and on the floor of the House of Representatives, a passageway ran down the center of each floor from end to end. Small cells, eight feet square, lined the sides of the passageways. Crowded inside were too many men, women and small children, Black and White—debtors, minor criminals, people waiting for trial and accused runaway slaves.

Nancy was led to a cell on the lower floor. It had no bed, chair or stool. She and the others slept on the damp brick floor on dirty blankets. In a corner was a hole through the floor leading to a large, open sewer underneath. Another hole in the cell above drained down through Nancy's wall to the sewer below. The stench was sickening, even when the holes were not clogged up.

At that time, Nancy had no way to let anyone know where she was. As May became June and June became steamy July, no one came for Nancy.

In July, the jailer ran an ad in a local paper, a copy of which is in the court files: "NOTICE. Will be sold at the Prison of Washington, 24th August 1835, a Negro Girl, who calls herself NANCY JONES."

Still, no one came.

While Nancy was in jail, an event took place in Washington that illustrates another precarious aspect of the "free" African Americans' existence then. On a mid-August night, a White man was brought to the jail for handing out pamphlets urging enslaved people to rebel. White people all over the city were reminded of the revolt of the enslaved in Virginia four years earlier led by an enslaved man named Nat Turner. During the revolt, enslaved African Americans killed White men, women and children, and Whites killed more than one hundred African Americans.

A night later, a crowd gathered near the jail, demanding the pamphleteer. But armed citizens surrounded the jail to protect it, and the crowd soon left.

The following day, however, local newspapers reported that four or five hundred men had wrecked two African American schoolhouses and ransacked a restaurant on Sixth Street owned by a free Black man named Beverly Snow and reported to be "much frequented by the good society of Washington." Yet the rioters said Snow had insulted some White women. Snow denied this (it was unlikely to be true), but he wisely fled town for his safety.

Time drew nearer for Nancy's sale, but fortunately, the jailer's ad was noticed. The day of the sale, a lawyer filed a petition for Nancy's release.

Three days later, Mullinix and a friend testified in court before Chief Judge William Cranch. Nancy was released and returned to Baltimore.

The court files show that only a few days after Nancy was arrested, Mullinix and Nancy's father signed an agreement that made Nancy Mullinix's apprentice for four years. She was to learn "the trade and mystery of a House servant and cook," and during this time, she was obligated "his lawful commands everywhere readily to obey" and not to "haunt ale houses, taverns, or playhouses." These were standard terms in apprentice agreements then, and many free African Americans became apprentices in similar fashion.

This apprenticeship undoubtedly made Mullinix more interested in coming to Washington for Nancy. Also, Nancy may have originally gone to Washington because she knew she was to become Mullinix's apprentice, didn't like it and ran away. After her release, perhaps she found that being someone's apprentice was better than being someone's slave. On the other hand, perhaps she found it was much the same.

Chapter 7

THE CIVIL WAR COMES
TO DUKE STREET

On May 24, 1861, at the very beginning of the Civil War in Virginia, the Union army invaded Alexandria. A familiar story of what happened on that day over 150 years ago concerns Union colonel Elmer Ellsworth, who led the Eleventh New York Volunteer Infantry Regiment, known as the Fire Zouaves, across the Potomac River by boat and into Alexandria. A short time after they landed, Ellsworth was shot and killed after lowering the Confederate flag from the top of the Marshall House Hotel on King Street, and then his killer, Confederate sympathizer James Jackson, was himself shot and killed by one of Ellsworth's men.

Although less well known, much else happened that day in Alexandria besides the confrontation between Ellsworth and Jackson. Involved in other striking incidents were the Confederate forces stationed in Alexandria, a different Union force that came to Alexandria by land, a Union naval contingent that entered Alexandria with an unexpected offer for the Confederates and a company of Zouaves acting separately from Ellsworth and the rest of his regiment. Interaction among these bodies resulted in a confrontation that took place out west on Duke Street that was almost as dramatic as the one between Ellsworth and Jackson.

THE INVASION BEGINS

Shortly before two o'clock on the morning of the twenty-fourth, Union soldiers began to march from the District of Columbia into Virginia across three bridges: the Long (a wooden bridge located generally where the Fourteenth Street Bridge is now), the Aqueduct (located close to where Key Bridge is now) and the Chain. Soldiers, cavalry horses and horses pulling artillery stepped out across the bridges on a night reported to be "particularly clear, and the moon…full and lustrous." Once across, they fanned out under orders to take control of Alexandria, Arlington Heights and other parts of rebellious northern Virginia.

One of the units ordered to march into Virginia over the Long Bridge early that morning was the First Michigan Volunteer Infantry, led by Colonel Orlando B. Willcox. Colonel Willcox was a thirty-eight-year-old West Point–trained officer from frontier-era Michigan who had served in both the Seminole War and the Mexican War and, as a young officer, had chased buffalo and Indians across the Great Plains. The force he led was composed of not only the First Michigan Volunteer Infantry Regiment but also a cavalry troop and a section of artillery consisting of two horse-drawn

Union soldiers march across the Long Bridge, early morning, May 24, 1861. *Harper's Weekly*.

Left: Colonel Orlando B. Willcox. *National Archives.*

Right: Colonel Elmer Ellsworth. *Harper's Weekly.*

cannons—a total of over one thousand men. Their mission, shared with Colonel Ellsworth's regiment, was to take control of Alexandria.

A number of other Union army units crossed the Long Bridge before it was the turn of Willcox and his soldiers. Once Wilcox and his men were over the bridge into Virginia, they turned left toward Alexandria. At a time when Union soldiers wore a great variety of uniforms, the Michigan First already wore the dark blue uniform with blue forage cap that later would become familiar as the official uniform of the Union army.

Marching cautiously, they approached Four Mile Run shortly after four o'clock in the morning. Across the creek on a hill, they saw several Confederate sentries mounted on horseback. As they watched, the Confederates quickly rode off in the direction of Alexandria.

Unfazed, Willcox and his men continued to the creek, where Willcox ordered a halt. He and Colonel Ellsworth had been instructed to meet each other there and, by exchanging signals, coordinate their entry into Alexandria so that they arrived at the same time.

Meanwhile, as Union soldiers began marching across bridges into Virginia, three steamboats and a variety of smaller boats chartered to the United States Navy arrived at Giesboro Point in the District of Columbia near the mouth of the Anacostia River. There, under Colonel Elmer Ellsworth's directions, the Eleventh New York Volunteer Infantry Regiment, better known as the New York Fire Zouaves (pronounced "Zoo-aahvs"), boarded the small boats that would take them out to the steamers for transportation across the Potomac to Alexandria.

One of the Zouaves boarding was Private Harrison Comings. In his mid-twenties, he was a four-year veteran of the New York Fire Department and a member of Company E, a unit of the Fire Zouaves that would play a distinctive role in the coming invasion of Alexandria. He also was an enthusiastic patriot. In fact, young Comings had his hair cut short and in such a way that it outlined an eagle on top of his head.

The small boats spent nearly two hours ferrying the approximately one thousand men from the shore to the steamers, where they crowded on board, finding space as best they could. Around four o'clock in the morning, the huge paddlewheels of the steamers began to revolve, and the four-and-a-half-mile trip down the Potomac River to Alexandria began.

The overloaded boats moved slowly downriver. Before long, they reached Four Mile Run, but Colonel Willcox, sitting stationary on his horse, watched from the shore as the steamboats passed by without a signal. Apparently, Ellsworth, in his eagerness to get to Alexandria, forgot—or simply ignored—his orders to coordinate with Willcox. After the boats had passed, Willcox simply ordered his men on to Alexandria. They would meet with the Zouaves when and where they could.

CONFEDERATES REACT

The Confederates stationed in Alexandria, however, were not surprised by the Union soldiers. Shortly after Union forces first began to cross over into Virginia, a mounted sentry who had been stationed near the Chain Bridge reported to Captain Mottrom Dulany Ball of the Confederate cavalry in Alexandria that Union cavalry units were advancing across the bridge. Captain Ball immediately informed Colonel George H. Terrett, a fifty-four-year-old former brevet major in the United States Marine Corps from Fairfax County, who commanded the Confederate forces in Alexandria. As Terrett later wrote, he ordered his men, who were quartered in several places in the city, to be roused from their beds, arm themselves and stand by for further orders.

Terrett's command consisted of five infantry companies from Alexandria—the Alexandria Riflemen, Mount Vernon Guards, Old Dominion Rifles, Emmett Guards and O'Connell Guards—and two cavalry troops under Captain Ball and Captain E.B. Powell. He may also have had under him other infantry companies from nearby parts of Virginia. Altogether, they totaled some five hundred men, considerably fewer than the Union forces headed their way.

Colonel Terret himself was a veteran officer with a colorful past. In his younger days, he fought a duel at Harper's Ferry with a U.S. Treasury Department official and emerged unscathed, shooting his opponent through both legs. In the Mexican War, he had behaved courageously, leading a company of marines in storming the walls of Chapultepec Castle (the renowned "Halls of Montezuma"). He had been in command at Alexandria, however, for only two weeks, having taken command on May 10 after the previous commanding officer was relieved in disgrace.

Just before dawn, Terrett received further word of the advancing Union force—this time, apparently, from the mounted sentries posted near Four Mile Run who had hurriedly reported that Union soldiers (Willcox's men) were approaching the creek and headed toward Alexandria. Terrett immediately sent word to his units scattered throughout the city to assemble at the prearranged rendezvous at the intersection of Washington and Prince Streets.

Apparently, some units had not received the earlier order to arm themselves and stand by. When this second word came, as Private John Zimmerman, a twenty-three-year-old former clerk at a dry goods store in Alexandria, later wrote,

> *We were aroused & ordered to pack up & fall in immediately—instantly all was commotion in the barracks—officers hurrying the men & men hastily dressing, packing knapsacks & blankets, seizing arms & accoutrements, & getting into line—no time was lost and in a few minutes we were moving at quick step to our rendezvous, the Lyceum, SW cor Prince & Washington Sts.*

THE U.S. NAVY ENTERS

At this time another, unexpected, player assumed a role in the developing Alexandria drama. The USS *Pawnee*, a gunboat carrying a full broadside of twenty-four-pound guns, had been stationed off the Alexandria docks for over three weeks. Shortly after four o'clock on the morning of the invasion, its commander, fifty-two-year-old Commodore Stephen C. Rowan of the U.S. Navy, another Mexican War veteran, looked upriver from the deck of his ship and saw Ellsworth's steamboats approaching him on their way to Alexandria. Concerned for the safety of Alexandria's women and children, Commodore Rowan dispatched Lieutenant R.B. Lowry ashore to find the Confederate commander in Alexandria and demand that he surrender the city. In doing so, however, Commodore Rowan acted without orders and completely on his own. His act was not part of the Union's invasion plan.

Lieutenant Lowry, as he later reported, found Colonel Terrett "in the open street, surrounded by excited soldiers." He informed Terret that, in Terrett's words, "an overwhelming force was about entering the city of Alexandria, and it would be madness to resist." There are some discrepancies between what Terrett and Lowry later reported concerning their conversation, but it appears as though Lowry gave Terrett several hours, until eight or nine o'clock in the morning, to surrender, evacuate or face hostilities. Certainly, that is what Terrett wrote he understood. Then Lowry returned to the Alexandria dock and the *Pawnee* just as light began spreading across the sky.

Back at the intersection of Washington and Prince, the veteran Terrett took stock of his situation as his troops continued to assemble. He had the offer from Lieutenant Lowry, and he knew the *Pawnee* had its guns trained on the city. He also had just learned from sentries, who had been stationed at the dock and now had reported to him, that Ellsworth's forces were approaching. Then he looked north out Washington Street and saw additional Union troops (Willcox's skirmishers) approaching the city. An additional factor in his consideration was that, ten days earlier, he had received a letter from General Robert E. Lee, commander of all Virginia forces, indicating that Lee did not believe it possible that Terrett "would be able to resist successfully an attempt to occupy Alexandria."

Terrett decided he could not wait until the time indicated by the *Pawnee* naval officer. Now was the time to evacuate. Once out of Alexandria, he hoped to find railroad cars waiting to take him and his men on to Manassas Junction, some thirty-five miles from Alexandria.

Even though all his men had not reached the assembly point, Terrett quickly gave the commands "Right face—quick right—forward march," and those soldiers who had assembled marched over to Duke Street and out Duke Street toward the edge of town. As they marched out Duke, Private

Private Edgar Warfield. *A Confederate Soldier's Memoir, 1936.*

John Zimmerman, the former dry goods store clerk, passed his house and saw "my mother & Bro & Sisters at the door and waving us on."

One company almost did not make it out of town with the rest of the Confederate soldiers. The quarters of the Old Dominion Rifles were out Cameron Street across from today's Jefferson-Houston School, and through a misunderstanding, they did not get the order to assemble when other companies did. When they did learn of the order, they hastily formed up and began marching down King Street to the assembly point. On their way—as Private Edgar Warfield, a member of the company, later remembered—two small boys excitedly told them that the other companies already had marched out Duke Street. The Rifles hurriedly changed direction and managed to catch up with the rest of the Alexandria

Confederates, but not until they were some distance from the city. There, the Confederates found trains that, each night, had been sent away from Alexandria to prevent their capture. Promptly, the excited but weary soldiers climbed on board the train's cars and were taken to Manassas to fight another day.

Earlier, as Terrett had led his Confederate soldiers out Duke Street on horseback, Captain Dulaney Ball rode with him. Terrett ordered Ball's and Powell's cavalry units to bring up the rear of the march and keep him informed of the enemy's progress.

On their way out Duke Street, Terrett and Ball passed the Orange and Alexandria Railway depot at Duke and Henry Streets. Soon afterward, they reached the quarters of Ball's cavalry troop in the 1300 block of Duke near the Price, Birch & Company slave pen and the corner of Duke and Payne Streets. Here, Captain Ball left the rest of the Confederates and rode over to his unit's barracks. Ball was a twenty-six-year-old graduate of William and Mary who had been until recently "a talented and witty schoolmaster" in Fairfax County. Slowly he began to assemble his troops, some forty officers and men—too slowly, as it turned out.

THE ZOUAVES ARRIVE

As the Confederates were leaving town, the lead steamboat carrying Ellsworth and his regiment of Fire Zouaves docked at the pier at the foot of Cameron Street and began disembarking the Zouaves. Each Zouave wore a bright red fireman's shirt tucked into baggy gray pants and partially covered by a short gray jacket lined with red. On each head was a red forage cap.

First to disembark from the boats was Company E. It consisted of about one hundred riflemen, including Private Harrison Comings with the shaved eagle on his head. Ellsworth immediately ordered the company to proceed at the double-quick march to the Orange and Alexandria Railroad depot to secure the railroad, tear up track and seize what rolling stock it could find. Shortly after giving the order, Ellsworth led a small party of men into Alexandria and on to his death at the Marshall House Hotel.

Meanwhile, Company E proceeded on its mission. Following the Orange and Alexandria train tracks along Union Street, Private Comings and his fellow Zouaves proceeded cautiously through, or perhaps around, the Wilkes

New York Fire Zouave. *Library of Congress*.

A cannon pointed straight at them. *Mathew Brady.*

Street tunnel and on west along the tracks on Wilkes Street. With no guide, they were proceeding into the unknown.

Before long, the tracks led them to the extensive O&A rail yard beginning at Wolfe and Henry Streets. Private Comings later wrote that when the Zouaves came in sight of the yard, their captain quickly ordered them to surround it. As some of the soldiers still were moving off to their positions, one of the first to leave returned quickly to report that rebel cavalrymen were forming two streets over. (This was Ball's troop on Duke Street.)

The captain ordered E Company to fall in. Once formed, he ordered them to double-quick march north on Henry Street toward Duke. As they turned the corner onto Duke, Private Comings looked west and saw Ball's cavalry in front of their quarters. Then, hearing a loud rumbling noise, he glanced to the east, down Duke, and saw, to his surprise, a cannon pointed straight at his company, "evidently with the intention of sending us to Kingdom Come without any warning," Comings later wrote. "Our captain made the remark to us that we had better make our peace with God, as our time had come."

Enter Willcox and Michigan

Several minutes earlier, Colonel Willcox and his soldiers had entered Alexandria from the north by Washington Street "in the midst of a glorious sunrise." Unlike the Zouaves, Willcox was not going completely into the unknown—he actually was somewhat familiar with Alexandria. Nine years earlier, he had been stationed at Fort Washington across the river in Maryland and had visited the city from time to time. Also, he had with him a guide, a Captain Owen from the District of Columbia cavalry. Willcox sent Owen on ahead to find out what was happening further into town. Soon, Owen returned to report that a troop of rebel cavalry was forming up on Duke Street.

Willcox was unaware that the naval commander of the *Pawnee* had led the Confederates to believe they could leave unmolested if they left before sometime later in the morning. He was then at the intersection of King and Washington Streets, two blocks north of Duke Street. Sitting straight on his horse, he called up his two cannons.

Each two-wheeled cannon was attached to the rear of a two-wheeled cart called a limber, resulting in a four-wheeled cart with the cannon facing backward. This combined cart was pulled by four or six horses hitched to its front in twos. Willcox's cannons were manned not by volunteers serving for a limited time but by regular army soldiers. A cannoneer rode on each of the left-side horses, and other cannoneers usually rode seated on ammunition boxes on the limber.

Willcox rode with his cannons up King Street, led them onto a cross street and continued the two blocks south to Duke. As they came to Duke Street, Willcox directed one of the horse-drawn cannons out onto the dirt of Duke. There, the horses quickly wheeled it around to point it up the street toward the rebel cavalry. At almost the same moment that the cannoneers unhooked the limber and horses from the cannon and prepared to fire, Private Comings and Zouave Company E marched onto Duke Street between Wilcox and the Confederate cavalry, saw the cavalry in one direction and an unfamiliar cannon aiming at them in the other and thought their time was up.

Before anyone could open fire, Colonel Willcox recognized the Zouaves as friendly, rode up to them and told them to stand by. He then rode on toward the startled Captain Ball, whose men, Wilcox later wrote, "seemed paralyzed; most of them were in the saddle while others stood stock still with one foot in the stirrup." Willcox yelled, "Surrender or I'll blow you to Hell!"

Captain Ball promptly handed over his sword. Willcox quickly ordered the Zouaves to surround the cavalry, disarm them, take them to the nearby slave pen and keep them there.

As Willcox and the Zouaves secured the captured Confederate cavalrymen, they received what Willcox later described as the "shocking news" that Ellsworth had been shot and was dead.

Willcox left the Zouaves to guard the Confederates and proceeded to secure the railway depot with his Michigan men. He then went to the telegraph office, where he met the new commander of the Zouaves, who told him that he had telegraphed Washington of Ellsworth's death. He also informed Willcox that the rest of the city was secure. Willcox then proudly telegraphed his superiors in Washington: "Alexandria is ours."

POSTSCRIPT

After the Zouaves placed the surrendered Confederate cavalrymen in the wall-enclosed yard of the slave pen, Private Comings and a few others went into one of the buildings also enclosed in the yard.

Here, they found a Black man chained to a ring on the floor in one of the building's rooms. He said he was a runaway and asked them who they were. When they answered they were Yankees and going to release him, he was elated.

Somewhat later, when soldiers of the First Michigan replaced the Fire Zouaves as guards at the slave jail, Colonel Willcox visited there. He found the auctioneer's account book with descriptions of enslaved people, their owners' names and the prices at which they were bought and sold. Some of the Michigan soldiers reported to him that they had found three enslaved people imprisoned there: a man, a girl and a boy. As they were freeing them, Willcox later wrote, "a well-dressed gentleman came to 'claim his property,' the negro man, whom he grabbed by the collar and attempted to take with him." Instead, "the master was hustled off alone amid the jeers of the Michigan men," and the former enslaved man "took free service" and became a cook in one of the Michigan companies. After the war, he traveled to Michigan with a captain of the First Michigan, in whose home he later passed away.

What the Zouaves and the Michigan men did in freeing the enslaved then actually was against the law. The Fugitive Slave Act enacted in 1850 punished

Union soldiers on guard at the Alexandria Slave Pen. *Library of Congress.*

anyone who harbored a fugitive slave and thus deprived the slave's owner of what, at that time, was considered the slave owner's property. Union general Butler had not yet announced his "contraband" doctrine, which considered Confederate enslaved "contraband of war" to be legitimately kept from helping their rebellious masters. That doctrine was not approved by the Lincoln administration until later in 1861. The New York and Michigan soldiers acted spontaneously based on their own basic sense of what was right and what was wrong.

CONCLUSION

The events on May 24, 1861, over 150 years ago, were more complex than perhaps many have realized. Instead of one invading unit arriving in Alexandria by water with a resulting tragedy, there was another invader arriving by land. In addition, there was the complicating factor of the surrender offer from the commander of the *Pawnee*; the difficult decision made by the commander of the Confederate forces, leading to their retreating to fight another day; the slow assembly and ignominious capture of Ball's Confederate cavalry; and one of the earliest instances of Union troops freeing Confederate enslaved.

Everyone involved in the invasion that day certainly learned that events in war do not always go according to plan.

EPILOGUE

Private Comings and the Zouaves

After May 24, most of the Fire Zouaves were stationed on Shuter's Hill. Here, they were put to work building the first Union fort to protect Alexandria, Fort Ellsworth. While others in the regiment worked on the fort, Private Comings and Company E were ordered into Alexandria to work with the Quartermaster Department guarding the quartermaster's stores.

Two months after the invasion of Alexandria, the Zouave regiment fought in the First Battle of Manassas. At that battle, Private Comings was knocked unconscious by a member of Jeb Stuart's Confederate cavalry and thought dead. Two days after the battle, however, after a long walk from the battlefield, he rejoined the Zouaves in Alexandria.

The Fire Zouaves were disbanded in the summer of 1862. Comings transferred to a Connecticut unit, and he was severely wounded at the Battle of Fredericksburg. After the war, he became a police officer and later chief of police of Malden, Massachusetts, where he died in 1893.

Captain of the USS Pawnee

Commodore Stephen Clegg Rowan, captain of the *Pawnee*, received a written reprimand from Secretary of the Navy Gideon Welles for his unauthorized "interference" in the secret movement on Alexandria. "In demanding the surrender of the town when the expedition from Washington was secretly approaching it, you committed, to say the least, a grave error."

However, Commodore Rowan's career survived the reprimand, and in fact, it prospered. He participated in General Burnside's invasion of eastern North Carolina in 1862, when he led thirteen steamers in an attack on a fleet of Confederate ships in the Pasquotank River in which the whole

Confederate fleet was captured or destroyed. He also participated in the siege of Charleston. He obtained the rank of vice admiral and died in 1890 at the age of eighty-one.

Alexandria Confederates

While camped in the Manassas and Bull Run area, the Alexandria Confederate infantry units were combined with infantry units from other parts of northern Virginia into the Seventeenth Virginia Infantry Regiment. This unit fought in numerous Civil War battles, from the First Battle of Manassas to Appomattox.

Privates Zimmerman and Warfield fought in many of those battles and survived the war. After the war, John Zimmerman became a wholesale coal merchant in Alexandria and died in 1926 at the age of eighty-seven. Edgar Warfield became a druggist in Alexandria and died in 1934 at the age of ninety-two, the last survivor of those who marched out of Alexandria on May 24, 1961.

Colonel George H. Terret was initially elevated to the command of a brigade at Manassas, but before the battle took place, he yielded his command to General James Longstreet, who outranked him, when Longstreet arrived in Manassas. Terret was then placed in charge of the heavy artillery defending the rear position of the Confederate army. He later returned to the marines, this time the Confederate States Marine Corps, and later commanded the fortifications at Drewery's Bluff. Four days before Lee surrendered, Terrett was captured leading a unit toward Appomattox. He was released on July 25, 1865, and died ten years later in Fairfax County at the age of sixty-eight.

Captain Mottrom Dulany Ball and his cavalry unit were released in June only after they pledged in writing not to take up arms against the United States again. Ball's signing this pledge and his apparent negligence in being captured in Alexandria were very controversial in the South. In September 1862, however, he was formally exchanged in a general prisoner exchange (even though he was not then a prisoner), which permitted him to fight again for the South. He then served in the Confederate army with distinction, commanding the Eleventh Virginia Cavalry Regiment and rising to the rank of lieutenant colonel. He was wounded twice, at Brandy Station and Toms Creek. After the war, he practiced law in Fairfax County for several years. In 1878, he was appointed collector of customs for the Territory of Alaska and moved to Sitka, Alaska. At that time, the holder of that office was the chief representative of the U.S. government in Alaska. He also served as Alaska's first unofficial delegate to Congress. He died in 1887 at the age of fifty-four on board ship heading back to Virginia.

Colonel Orlando B. Willcox and the First Michigan Volunteers

In the reorganization of the Union army before the First Battle of Manassas, Colonel Willcox was given expanded responsibilities as the commander of the Second Brigade of the Third Division. His brigade consisted of four regiments, including his old regiment, the First Michigan Volunteers, and the Eleventh New York Volunteers (the Fire Zouaves). Colonel Willcox's Brigade fought in the crucial part of the Manassas battle. Willcox himself behaved bravely, was wounded and was captured. On August 16, 1862, he was exchanged and immediately promoted to brigadier general. He later led units in several important battles, including Antietam, Fredericksburg, the Wilderness and the Crater.

After the war, Willcox remained in the army and served in several posts, including a posting to Whipple Barracks in Prescott, Arizona, in 1878, which resulted in his leading units in fights with the Chiricahua Apaches. He died in 1907 at the age of eighty-four. In 1895, he received the Congressional Medal of Honor for his actions at the First Battle of Manassas.

Chapter 8

A HISTORY OF DEL RAY

1894 to Today

W hat has now become one of the most desirable places to live in northern Virginia, the area within Alexandria known as Del Ray, was not only one of the earliest commuter suburbs near Alexandria but also once a separate town with a Main Street that was typical of small-town America (parts of it still exist today). Moreover, it was the residence of several colorful individuals, the location of a notorious gambling facility, the site of a 1920s bank robbery and the scene of other elements of a colorful but little-known history.

ESTABLISHMENT

Its story begins in 1894, about thirty years after the end of the Civil War. The area that is now Del Ray was then outside of the boundaries of the city of Alexandria and in what was called Alexandria (now Arlington) County.

The area was mainly farmland. Along its eastern edge was the Washington-Alexandria Turnpike, now US 1. Stretching across this farmland were the tracks of a railroad, the old Alexandria, Loudoun and Hampshire line, which ran in a northwesterly direction from Alexandria, across the turnpike and farmland and eventually to Leesburg, Virginia, and beyond.

In that year, 1894, plans were being made to build a streetcar line that would run from Washington through Alexandria and on to George Washington's

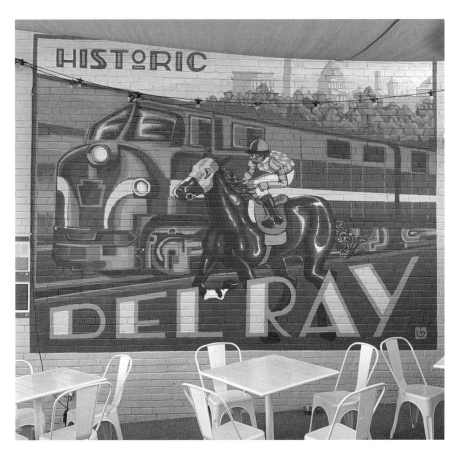

Del Ray mural on the side of Cheestique, 2411 Mount Vernon Avenue. *Author's collection.*

Mount Vernon. The part of the line running between Washington and Alexandria would cross Four Mile Run just beyond today's Cora Kelley School, at what is now the end of Commonwealth Avenue. From there, it would proceed down the middle of what would become Commonwealth Avenue to King Street and on farther south.

In 1894, the horse-and-buggy days before automobiles, two developers from Cincinnati, Ohio, Charles E. Wood and William Harmon, realized that land alongside this planned streetcar line would be a perfect place for families to live. From homes there, fathers, mothers and their children could board the streetcar and ride easily into D.C. for work, shopping or entertainment.

Thus, Wood and Harmon bought this property and laid out two subdivisions, St. Elmo to the north and Del Ray to the south. Between the two subdivisions was a horse racetrack called the Alexandria Gentlemen's Driving Club, about which more follows later.

St. Elmo was named after the patron saint of sailors and was the smaller of the two subdivisions. It had 491 long, narrow lots. The lots were 25 feet in front, along the street, and extended away from the street 105 feet. St. Elmo was bordered on the east by the Washington-Alexandria Turnpike (US 1) and on the north by what now are Glebe Road and Ashby Street. Its western border was the old Alexandria, Loudoun and Hampshire Railroad, whose route is clearly visible today. The tracks have been removed, and a person can walk along the old roadbed, starting at US 1 just behind the Del Ray Animal Hospital on Mount Ida Avenue, in a northwesterly direction all the way to Commonwealth Avenue.

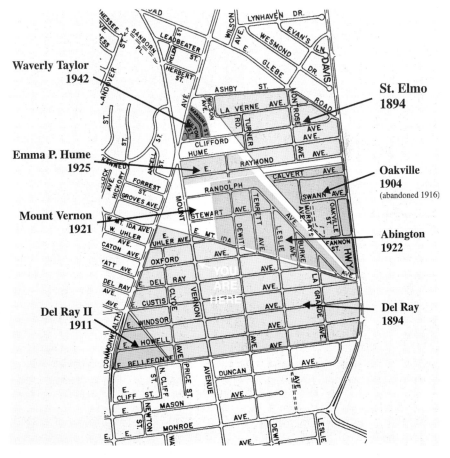

Map of Town of Potomac showing original St. Elmo and Del Ray developments. *Leland Ness.*

Del Ray was the larger of the two subdivisions. It contained 1,160 lots of the same long, narrow size and stretched from what would become Commonwealth Avenue to US 1 and from Bellefonte Avenue to Mount Ida Avenue.

By 1905, eleven years after the subdivisions opened, Wood, Harmon & Company had sold 62 percent of the lots in both subdivisions. The average price of a lot was $143.

Racetrack

While the subdivisions were selling lots and building houses, the Alexandria Gentlemen's Driving Club, better known as the St. Asaph Track, was constructing its horse racetrack between the two subdivisions. When finished, its grandstand held five thousand spectators and accommodated forty bookmakers. Its three-quarter-mile oval track stretched from close to US 1 along Mount Ida Avenue almost to Mount Vernon Avenue, with stables for horses located on both sides of Mount Vernon Avenue.

When construction was completed in late 1894, the racetrack quickly became tremendously popular. This popularity continued, even though the *Alexandria Gazette* reported such shameful activities at the track as fastening lead shoes to the horses to make them run slower. In 1897, however, Virginia outlawed betting on horse races. This legislation ensured that races at the track were no longer profitable, and they ceased.

However, the most popular part of the St. Asaph operation always had been betting on races that took place out of state, at such places as the track in Saratoga, New York. These bets were placed in part of the grandstand called the poolroom. (At St. Asaph's, a poolroom was not a place for playing billiards but a place for placing bets.) That aspect of the operation continued after races at the track were outlawed.

To make the betting at least arguably legal, a private telegraph line ran from the St. Asaph Track poolroom to Harpers Ferry, West Virginia, where horse race betting was legal. Bets were recorded and money collected at the St. Asaph poolroom. They then were transferred over the telegraph wire to a group in Harpers Ferry called the West Virginia Athletic Association. The athletic association then placed the bets and later reported the results back to the poolroom. Thus, the poolroom operators claimed that the bets were placed legally in West Virginia.

Old grandstand at the St. Asaph's racetrack. *Rita Holtz Collection.*

The poolroom probably looked something like the betting room in the 1973 movie with Paul Newman and Robert Redford called *The Sting*. At St. Asaph, as in the movie, an operator sitting at a telegraph ticker passed racing information to men called runners. The runners then walked quickly across the room and passed the information to slickly dressed men standing on a stage beside long blackboards. Onto the blackboards, which bettors could easily see, the men wrote the names of racing entries, betting odds and race results. After learning whether his horse won or lost, a bettor could walk to another part of the grandstand and buy a drink (and celebrate or drown his sorrows) at the Hiawatha Pleasure and Social Club. It was a very efficient operation.

Citizens of St. Elmo and Del Ray and elsewhere in the county disliked the crowds the poolroom drew, feared it also attracted crime and complained loudly about such an immoral, illegal and distasteful operation. In 1902, the county managed to elect a crusading commonwealth attorney named Crandall Mackey. Mackey aimed to shut the poolroom down. He continually pressed charges against the poolroom operators. Yet Alexandria claimed police jurisdiction over the poolroom, and either the Alexandria police refused to serve Mackey's warrants or the city court dismissed the charges Mackey brought. In 1904, the poolroom was said to be making $150,000 a year in profit, so it easily could afford some $12,000 a year in alleged graft to local Alexandria officials.

Finally, however, in January 1905, an independent-minded commonwealth attorney in Alexandria named S.G. Brent prepared warrants against the poolroom himself. Then, on his own, he quietly ordered the Alexandria police to raid the offending institution.

The poolroom received no warning, and the raid was successful, resulting in the arrest of all poolroom employees. In the ensuing court case, the manager of the poolroom's telegraph operation was convicted of illegal betting, fined $200 and sentenced to six months in jail.

The poolroom closed when all its employees were arrested. After the conviction, it never reopened.

INCORPORATION

In 1906, the citizens of St. Elmo and Del Ray were free of the blight of the racetrack, and things were looking up. That same year, the railroad switching facility of Potomac Yard opened across US 1, bringing with it new residents for the two subdivisions. In addition, the streetcar line down Commonwealth Avenue was extremely successful, running thirty electric trains a day, carrying 1,743,734 people a year.

Still, not many subdivision lots actually had buildings on them, and the citizens of St. Elmo and Del Ray thought they could obtain better municipal services and attract more people if they were incorporated.

Thus, in January 1908, the five hundred citizens of the two subdivisions applied to the Virginia legislature for incorporation. The legislature was sympathetic, and on March 13, 1908, the subdivisions were officially incorporated as the Town of Potomac.

Over the next several years, electric lighting was installed, sewer and water service was improved and Mount Vernon Avenue was paved. In 1921 and 1922, the old racetrack property was divided into lots and developed as two subdivisions within the Town of Potomac.

1920s BANK ROBBERY

The racetrack was no longer, but the town of Potomac was not crime-free. On May 4, 1929, a Saturday, at 10:05 a.m., five men walked into the Bank of Del Ray at 2018 Mt. Vernon Avenue (now the home of Thai Peppers restaurant) and carefully closed the door behind them.

While one remained guarding the door, three others immediately showed their revolvers to the tellers standing at their windows. As two held their guns on the tellers, the third pocketed his gun, jumped over a barricade to the tellers' cash drawers and began filling his leather hand-satchel with cash. Meanwhile, the fifth man walked over and ripped out the telephone wires.

Outside, a sixth man waited in the getaway car.

None wore a mask. All appeared to be between thirty and thirty-five years old, and those who spoke did so with a foreign accent. All wore gray gloves in order to not leave fingerprints.

Only two employees were there, both tellers: Mr. C.E. Jones and Miss Mary Ford. According to the *Alexandria Gazette*, the two were told to "stick them up," which they quickly did. One of the gunmen then backed them up against the wall behind their stations and told them to keep quiet.

The only customer was twelve-year-old Ray Thomas of Mount Ida Avenue, sent by his parents to deposit twenty dollars. The robber who had ripped out the telephone wires quickly seized him and used the wires to bind the struggling boy.

Meanwhile, the robber with the satchel had grabbed cash out of the tellers' drawers and begun taking more from the large steel vault that was standing

Bank of Del Ray, 1920s. *Gallagher Collection, Alexandria Library, Special Collections.*

Bank of Del Ray building, now Thai Peppers restaurant. *Author's collection.*

open when they entered. As he worked, another customer, Fred L. Holt, came in to make a deposit. One of the gunmen immediately shoved the newcomer into the open vault, and another quickly added the tellers. When they tried to close the vault door, however, an open bolt caught against the doorframe and prevented its being secured.

Still, now satisfied, the robbers rapidly departed with their loot and made their getaway in a Buick sedan with D.C. plates driven by the sixth man. (This vehicle later was discovered to have been stolen.) The whole operation took less than ten minutes.

Despite no working phone, word quickly spread and a dozen policemen, many neighbors and a couple of reporters soon showed up. When questioned, Miss Ford avowed it was the first time in her life she had witnessed a bank holdup, although she admitted that she had read about many of them. Meanwhile, twelve-year-old Ray Thomas had managed to untangle himself from the telephone wires. He appeared not to be at all frightened and eagerly told a *Gazette* reporter all that had happened.

Later, the bank calculated the gunmen got away with $2,808.70—a professional job, the police said.

Two days later, still nothing had been seen of the robbers. Whether they ever were apprehended and punished is unknown.

ANNEXATION

The town of Potomac did not remain independent for long, however. At midnight on January 1, 1930, Alexandria officially annexed it.

The people of Potomac opposed the annexation. One Potomac council member said the town's citizens would sell their homes and move farther out into Arlington County: "We know Alexandria. We want none of it, and it shall have none of us."

Legend has it that the town was so opposed that it determined not to turn over its records to Alexandria, and one night, they were mysteriously burned.

Regardless, Potomac became part of Alexandria and soon became known as Del Ray. It contained then, and to a large extent still contains, a rich mixture of different housing styles, including precut homes from Sears and Roebuck Company, one- and one-and-a-half-story bungalows and four-square dwellings with large front porches.

MOUNT VERNON AVENUE IN THE 1940s

It might be interesting to take a brief look at some places along Mount Vernon Avenue, the main street of the Town of Potomac and now Del Ray's traditional Main Street, as they are today and as they were in the 1940s, shortly after Del Ray was annexed by Alexandria. It also might be interesting to glimpse something of how it was to be a kid in Del Ray some eighty years ago.

To start with, on the 2400 block on Mt. Vernon Avenue diagonally across from the Mount Vernon Community School playground is the long building that today has the Cut Piece restaurant on one end and Cheesetique on the other. In the 1940s, there was a similar building there with one odd difference—in the basement was a bowling alley called the Del Ray Recreation Center. There, pins were set by hand by local boys who were paid four cents a game for their work. Above the bowling alley, on the street level floor of the building, were the Del Ray Restaurant, the Monticello Beauty Shop, a Firestone tire store, a radio shop, the College Barber Shop and a couple of other stores. Above these commercial shops were apartments, where condos are now.

One freezing December morning in 1945, at the early hour of 2:20 a.m., the building caught fire. Quickly, the rising flames forced the thirteen families who lived in the upper-floor apartments to flee for their lives. As described in the *Alexandria Gazette*, men, women and children made "a mad dash into the [icy] streets…many still in their nightgowns and pajamas."

As regular and volunteer firemen and all the fire engines available in the city fought the fire, the local community rallied. Women volunteers of the Red Cross, Alexandria chapter, quickly arrived on the scene in a truck loaded with coffee and donuts for the firemen. The Hamilton Drug Store, 2400 Mt. Vernon Avenue (now Tops of Old Town), opened its heated store to help warm the freezing firemen, and the Mt. Vernon Barber Shop next door (now Del Ray Boccato) served hot coffee to the firemen. A city councilman even distributed cigars and cigarettes, and downtown in Alexandria itself, the local chapter of the U.S.O. opened its doors on South Washington Street for the apartment house evacuees.

Despite the firemen's "tireless efforts," the fire gutted the building and made all thirteen families homeless. The bowling alley and the stores on the ground floor were destroyed. All that remained of the building, according to the *Gazette*, was "a black yawning gap, filled with water and surrounded by tottering red brick walls on which hung thousands of icicles."

Despite the disaster, the building soon was rebuilt, looking much like the one destroyed by the fire. That building stands there today.

St. Elmo Pub's mural on the side of the pub, 2300 Mount Vernon Avenue. *Author's collection.*

Mighty Mo Kitchen in Leesburg, built like Del Ray's Mighty Midget. *Chris Wadsworth*.

Nearby, across the avenue, the building now occupied by Yoga in Daily Life was, in the 1940s, a movie theater called the Palm. On Saturday afternoons, kids in the neighborhood would enter to see westerns, catch the latest episode of a serial and learn whether the hero narrowly escaped this time.

An afternoon at the movies at the Palm cost eleven cents, including one cent tax. Once, the Palm showed on screen the real, live birth of a baby, and several people in the audience fainted.

Where St. Elmo's Coffee Pub is located was, in the 1940s, a children's clothing store. Next door, the UPS store was a women's dress store called the Scott Shoppe. Farther down the avenue, the building where the Junction is now was a Safeway grocery store.

One odd building in the late 1940s stood on the corner at the intersection of Mount Vernon and Mason Avenues (where a Hyundai parking lot is now). It was called the Mighty Midget, and it was a tiny metal building about the size of three telephone booths standing side by side, made from the fuselage of a World War II bomber.

The one person who could fit inside would serve passersby through its small window. Out the window would pass hamburgers, hot dogs, potato chips, ice cream sandwiches, candy bars and cold drinks. Kids walking along the avenue to school at George Washington would get a cupcake or candy bar as they passed in the morning and a cold drink coming back by in the afternoon.

1970s and 1980s

By this time, the Del Ray neighborhood, in the eyes of some, had begun to go downhill. In 2013, a longtime Del Ray resident listed on the Del Ray Association website some of the people living in the neighborhood in the mid-1980s. They included:

An escaped con named Dave who had walked off from a prison work detail and married a topless dancer. He used the street and his yard as an automobile junkyard and repair shop.

An ex-Arkansas bootlegger named Buck who had fled that state after burglarizing a liquor store. He once lived on the Potomac shore in cardboard boxes until his girlfriend, Bertha, convinced him to move into better quarters. Their dog was a large, mutant, unwashed Chihuahua who never went indoors and never met anyone he liked. Buck's backyard housed not only the dog but also fifteen black-and-white television sets.

A character named Socrates who, one Saturday night, got drunk in D.C. and led police of four jurisdictions on a rousing car chase, smashing into multiple parked vehicles in the process. The chase ended at three o'clock in the morning on East Mt. Ida when Socrates's girlfriend coaxed him down from the roof of his house, which was surrounded by police, by assuring him he wouldn't be shot.

A popular dive then was a bar and grill at 2400 B Mount Vernon Avenue called Mac's Place. There, one entered the front door into "smoke and grime, the smell of alcohol, and endless tedious tales of drunks trying to [drown] their broken dreams." (It now, however, is the popular Taqueria Poblano restaurant.)

Also living in Del Ray then were poor Black and poor White people; hardworking, blue-collar Blacks and Whites, many working at the railroad yard across US 1 from the neighborhood; and unpretentious middle-class men and women.

Del Ray then was characterized as "an edgy old authentic neighborhood with lots of funky charm and affordable houses."

UP TO DATE

Whereas the renovation of Old Town Alexandria began in the mid-1960s, renovation of the residential part of Del Ray began later, in the late 1970s.

Renovation of the commercial part of Del Ray began even later, with the establishment of St. Elmo's Coffee Pub in 1996. From that time, more and more attractive shops and restaurants have come to Del Ray, until today it is one of the most sought-after living areas in northern Virginia.

Chapter 9

BOOTS, SADDLES & TANKS

The U.S. Army's Horse Cavalry Between the World Wars

On June 15, 1930, a poised cadet from the Virginia Military Institute proudly drove his dilapidated old Ford through the gates of Fort Myer, Virginia, across the Potomac River from Washington, D.C., and home of the crack Third Cavalry Regiment.

A dozen years after World War I ended, Cadet Charlie Dayhuff and other Reserve Officer Training Corps cadets were beginning the six weeks of concentrated training given to men who wanted to be officers in the modern U.S. cavalry. Cadet Dayhuff was about to trade his car for a horse.

At the same time, the U.S. military at the highest levels was debating whether to trade its horses for cars—or for some form of mechanized vehicle. The horse cavalry had survived World War I and the 1920s. But by 1930, the debate over horse or machine had begun in earnest and would not conclude until after World War II had started.

The story of the horse cavalry between the wars involves well-known figures like John J. Pershing, George C. Marshall and George S. Patton Jr. (the latter's views may be surprising), and some lesser known, like Generals Adna R. Chaffee and John K Herr. It also involves men in much lower ranks, like Cadet Dayhuff and his fellow ROTC cadets, who were trained to fight the next war on horseback.

In the end, the cavalry lost its horses—but not until its supporters made a determined fight against the "sheep-like rush to mechanization," not until Cadet Dayhuff and his friends experienced what it was like to be a cavalryman and not until, on December 22, 1941, the U.S. horse cavalry met tanks in combat.

Cadets of the Virginia Military Institute urge their horses across a wintry stream. *Author's collection.*

WORLD WAR I

But first, the earlier war. A little after four o'clock on the afternoon of September 12, 1918, three hastily assembled troops of roughly three hundred horsemen of the U.S. Second Cavalry rode their mounts down a road through a thick wood in northern France. The cavalrymen were part of the attack on the St. Mihiel salient that had begun at dawn that day. Up to now, they had spent most of their time in France running remount depots for the medical corps, the artillery and the transportation service, all of which used horses to haul equipment. Now well behind the original German lines, they were riding ahead of their infantry for the first time. This was the U.S. cavalry's first chance for actual combat in World War I.

The cavalrymen rode through the forest in two columns, one on each side of the central road. Halfway through the woods, they suddenly confronted the most effective weapon of the war, the machine gun.

Fire came at them from the right front, from at least one machine gun and possibly several automatic rifles, but the trees were too thick to see for sure.

The cavalry commander quickly ordered the troopers to turn back down the road to dismount and then advance again. "The men were falling back… in good order, when suddenly [another] machine gun opened up on the column from a small trail leading from the main road on the right," wrote Captain Ernest N. Harmon, who was there. "The Germans had allowed our patrols to go by and had brought their guns to the edge of the woods as the column started back."

Their horses were culls from veterinary hospitals and remount depots— most completely new to working as cavalry mounts. This second machine gun proved too much. The inexperienced horses bolted down the road, carrying their riders with them. Then another machine gun opened up from a trail on their left. In the confusion, few troopers could check their horses. They burst from the same woods they had just entered and scattered out over a field. Finally, the cavalrymen regained control. Slowly, they rode back to their own lines.

Not only was this defeat the first combat experienced by the U.S. cavalry in the war, but it was also its last, at least by a force of any size. It was not an enviable record to carry into the peace that followed.

CAVALRYMEN DEFEND THEIR MOUNTS

Immediately after the war, General John J. Pershing, leader of the American Expeditionary Force, appointed a board of officers to recommend a new army structure. The board focused on creating chiefs for various branches— infantry, artillery, signal corps and so on—under a single chief of staff. The infantry clearly merited a separate branch chief. The air service was new but had proved its value. Tanks had some successes and some problems. What about the cavalry?

Cavalrymen pointed out several things. First, the war on the western front had been unique: it was a war without movement. The two sides simply faced each other and slugged it out for four years. No war had been fought like it before, and its great cost, huge number of casualties and yearslong stalemate would ensure that no nation would ever fight that way again.

Cavalrymen argued that their strength was their mobility. The usual battle progressed in three phases: first, two forces sought to locate each other; second, the forces struggled for dominance; and third, one side was quickly defeated and the other pursued it.

Cavalry was most valuable when war was fluid—during a battle's first (locating) and third (pursuit) phases. On the western front, the first and third phases had been brief. But the middle phase (struggle) had lasted four long years.

Cavalry was important in the middle phase also, the cavalrymen argued, but mainly on the flanks of a battle. On the western front, however, *there had been no flanks.* The west end of the line of trenches stretching across Europe rested on the sea and the east end on neutral Switzerland and the mountains. This situation would not recur, either.

Future wars would be wars of movement, when cavalry would be essential. Tanks had some success in the war, but they were slow. Neither the light tanks used by the United States (Renaults borrowed from the French) nor the heavy tanks (borrowed from the English) could move more than five or six miles per hour, even on a good road.

Off-road, tanks were even more deficient. The day the first Renaults were used by the Americans (during the St. Mihiel offensive), only 1 tank was lost to enemy fire, but 22 were lost to "ditching" (getting stuck in shell craters or trenches) and 21 to mechanical failure. Of the 142 tanks operated by the Americans on the first day of the Meuse-Argonne offensive, only 16 were

World War I tank in France. *Library of Congress.*

available for the last assault a week later—again largely due to ditching and mechanical failure, according to David E. Johnson in his book *Fast Tanks and Heavy Bombers*.

Also, tanks ran out of gas and could be refueled only when road-bound motorized vehicles could reach them. Moreover, tanks were deaf and blind. A soldier buttoned up in a World War I tank had no radio. To communicate with other tanks or with infantry, he had to open up and wave a signal flag. Of greater concern was that his vision was so impaired "that enemy gun crews usually found the tank before the tank found them," as J.L.S. Daley related in "From Theory to Practice: Tanks, Doctrine, and the U.S. Army."

Airplanes, cavalrymen asserted, were useful for long-range reconnaissance—if it was daylight and the weather was good. Airplane-to-ground communication generally was too poor for planes to be useful for short-range reconnaissance. They might be of some use supporting infantry and cavalry in the attack, but they could not take prisoners or occupy ground.

The all-weather, all-terrain, live-off-the-ground, fast, mobile horse cavalry was the force required.

Cavalrymen pointed to British success during the war with horse cavalry in Palestine. The Dorset yeomanry successfully charged Turks on a ridge near Jerusalem on November 13, 1917, reported an article in the *Cavalry Journal* published in 1920. The yeomanry rode across 4,000 yards of open plain, then 150 feet up a hill—all under heavy artillery, machine gun and rifle fire—overran the position and captured 1,096 prisoners, 2 field guns and 14 machine guns. Their losses were 129 cavalrymen killed and wounded and 150 horses.

"The weapon used was the sword," the article stated. It quoted a captured Turkish officer describing the charge: "We were amazed and alarmed, because we could not believe our eyes. We had been taught that such a thing was impossible…yet now we saw this very thing being done. We did not know what to do."

Cavalrymen were quick to point out that the terrain in Palestine was much like that along the U.S. border with Mexico, and during World War I, the U.S. cavalry had fought bandits in Mexico in 1916 before Americans fought Germans in Europe in 1917.

Just after the war, the cavalrymen had little opposition. Other branches were more concerned about preserving their own turf than attacking another's. In addition, Pershing's board needed little convincing. It was composed of high-ranking officers who had little front-line experience of the Great War—their positions were too senior, and the U.S. experience in France had been too short. They looked to the past, where there had always been cavalry. To almost no one's surprise, the board recommended that Congress include cavalry in new legislation as one of the combat arms.

If that was not sufficient for Congress, Pershing, who had led cavalry into Mexico in pursuit of Pancho Villa in 1916, intervened. He wrote just before final congressional action: "To some unthinking persons the day of the cavalry seems to have passed. Nothing could be farther from the truth. The splendid work of the [British and French] cavalry in the [first] few weeks of the war more than justified its existence and the expense of its upkeep in the years of peace preceding the war."

That was enough for Congress. The National Defense Act of 1920 created a separate chief for the cavalry as well as the other combat arms. Moreover, that same law placed the tank corps, which had been a separate branch during the war, firmly under control of the infantry.

The implications of this new army organization did not escape the attention of one army officer. Major George S. Patton Jr., a former cavalryman, had formed and led the first U.S. tank unit into combat during the war. He

George S. Patton and a World War I tank in France. *National Archives*.

realized, however, that a tank element subordinate to a much larger infantry branch offered little hope of personal advancement. He switched back to the cavalry and soon became one of its principal spokesmen. "In offensive and defensive actions in stabilized situations, as well as in warfare of movement," he wrote in the *Cavalry Journal*, the semiofficial publication of the U.S. cavalry, "modern Cavalry has proven its value."

The cavalry had survived. For a while, at least, the horse was safe. And if the cavalry was to help fight the nation's future battles, it needed a reserve of trained officers.

Cadets Saddle Up

So, at Fort Myer one June morning in 1930, Cadet Dayhuff and forty-seven other ROTC trainees (from VMI, Culver Military Academy and Dartmouth) marched down to the stables in their olive-green uniforms, wide-brimmed campaign hats and knee-high leather riding boots to choose their most important items of equipment for the next six weeks: their horses.

The stables were long, low buildings of red brick from which emanated the musty odor of horses and straw. Between the stables, the horses stood quietly, their bridles hitched to a long rope running between tall posts known as a picket line.

Dayhuff's father was a cavalry officer with the Fourth Cavalry at Fort Meade, South Dakota, and the junior Dayhuff knew horses. He chose a bay, while a friend, Louie Roberts, whose Norfolk, Virginia background gave him no similar experience, selected a small black horse. Roberts reasoned, "Small, so less horse to groom." But Dayhuff knew a bay horse sweats less than a black one and requires less grooming. Before long, Roberts knew it too.

Some trainees had learned at school not to pick a "herring-gutted" horse, either. The body of such a horse angled sharply back and up from its chest to its rear legs. A saddle cinched around the horse's thick chest soon worked backward and loosened. When a rider leaned too much on the right stirrup or on the left, he could suddenly find himself and his saddle underneath the horse.

Another VMI cadet, Eddie Pulliam, son of a commonwealth attorney from Richmond, Virginia, selected a beautiful big horse and found out too late it had only one good eye. "Try to jump a one-eyed horse," he said years

Left: Cavalry recruitment poster, 1920. *Library of Congress*.

Below: Horses on picket line at Fort Myer. *National Archives*.

later. "The first time he approached a jump, he looked at it real hard with the one blank eye, then the other—and then went around on the side."

The cadets learned later that their horses were normally assigned to the headquarters band and were not great cavalry mounts, even with two good eyes. One cadet claimed his bulky horse surely carried a baby grand piano, while another said his horse would not have carried a piccolo.

Once a cavalryman had his horse, what was he to do with it? Scout to find the enemy, screen friendly troop movements, delay an enemy's advance by darting thrusts and quick withdrawals, pursue the enemy after a breakthrough, maintain liaison with other units and seize enemy positions— all traditional cavalry roles.

Cavalry theory, as set forth in *Employment of Cavalry*, published in 1924 by the Cavalry School in Fort Riley, Kansas, acknowledged that at times, machine guns, artillery and tanks were useful—they could pin the enemy to the ground so that cavalry could take the offensive on the flanks.

Mainly, however, the Cavalry School stressed the cavalry's ability to take care of itself in a fight and to advance rapidly. A cavalryman could ride to a fight and then dismount, but he should strive to fight mounted. When dismounted, the cavalry's fighting force was reduced because some troopers needed to stay with the riderless horses. In the 1920s, the cavalry boosted its firepower by integrating machine-gun-carrying troops into its regiments.

The speed and spirit of the cavalry were emphasized. Mounted men would "strike so quickly as to take the enemy...before he can prepare to receive the attack" and then, "by the moral effect and speed of galloping horsemen, destroy the enemy's will to resist." Cavalrymen quoted an old maxim: "Victory is gained not by the number killed but the number frightened."

There was some debate over the most effective cavalry weapon. Some said it was the pistol. Others said that even a man lying behind a machine gun found it extremely unsettling to have the point of a sword bearing down on him at the speed of a horse and with the force of a horse and rider behind it. In 1922, Major Patton, then commander of the Third Squadron, Third Cavalry at Fort Myer, described the cavalryman's spirit in terms that left no doubt as to its value: "The fierce frenzy of hate and determination flashing from the bloodshot eyes squinting behind the glittering steel is what wins."

But these tactics were useless unless the cavalry had officers and men who were trained to ride, and ride well. At seven thirty each morning at Fort Myer, the bugle blew "Boots and Saddles," and the cavalry cadets saddled up for equitation classes: slow trotting, galloping, jumping and general horsemanship.

Cadets take a winter ride at VMI. *Author's collection.*

The trainees already knew the basics about riding, having learned them at school. This instruction started with the cadet simply sitting on the horse, holding the reins. It proceeded to gripping the horse with the legs, then prodding the horse from a walk to a trot, then the canter, the gallop, the left-leg lead and the right-leg lead. The goal, finally, was for each cadet to ride with ease and to jump with his reins knotted before the saddle, arms folded across his chest, feet out of the stirrups and campaign hat strapped over his eyes.

Squad, platoon and troop drills followed equitation. They were conducted on a dusty drill field, a half-mile long and a quarter-mile wide. These drills, like infantry drills, were ways of getting men and horses from one place to another in an orderly manner—column of twos (the usual march formation), column of fours and parade formations. The cadets also practiced changing from marching formation (column) to fighting formation (line). Occasionally the cadets might spread out in two long lines, one right behind the other, for a controlled charge.

At VMI, drill included practice with a cavalry saber, which was a heavy, perfectly straight blade almost three feet long (designed by young lieutenant

George S. Patton Jr. in 1913), rather than a curved, scimitar-shaped blade. When charging mounted troops, a cavalryman was to ride down on the enemy soldier with his saber thrust out ahead, arm stiff and rotated slightly inward, run the man through, then let the momentum of the horse pull the blade out as he continued ahead.

At Fort Myer, the riding drill would continue until ten o'clock in the morning and, at times, included long rides in the hot sun along the dusty roads of rural Virginia. Returning to the corral, the cadets were hot, thirsty and worn out. Their equipment was in foul shape, and the horses were lathered and covered with powdery dust. Then the real work began.

Even before getting a drink of water for himself, a cadet had to take care of his horse. First, he must take the saddle off, clean it and put it away. Then he had to walk his horse until it cooled down. Then came grooming. A cadet could not simply throw water on his horse to remove the dust. He had to go over the horse thoroughly with a metal-toothed currycomb, then stroke him with a good strong brush.

All of this usually took about an hour and a half. The grooming was hard labor, each cadet stripped to the waist in the hot morning air. Louie Roberts began to learn the drawbacks of a black horse. The labor was made easier, however, by a constant exchange of wisecracks and exaggerated tales of exploits in nearby Washington. A cadet was finished only after a sergeant inspected his horse and said he was finished. If the horse was not ready, the cadet had to go back over it again.

Once finished, a cadet could return to the tall, pyramid-shaped tent he shared with three other cadets, pick up a towel and walk over to the dispensary for a shower. Then came lunch at one of the red-brick barracks, where gallons of ice-cold lemonade and large quantities of usually good food were served.

IS MECHANIZED THE WAY TO GO?

The cadets used transportation other than horses on one field exercise. Automobiles modified to go off road (called scout cars) had recently been added to cavalry units for reconnaissance duties. The cadets wanted to try one, but the Fort Myer cavalry lacked the money to use it for this purpose. The cadets were curious enough about the car, however, that they chipped in for the gas and tried it out, having a great time driving more on-road than off.

M1 scout car, 1930s. *Wikimedia Commons.*

Meanwhile, like the cadets, the U.S. military was becoming curious about making greater use of mechanized vehicles. This included even the cavalry, to a limited extent. Besides scout cars, in the late 1920s, the cavalry also experimented with "portee cavalry": using trucks and other motor vehicles to transport horses and riders long distances. The idea was not to replace the horse with a machine but to save the horse for its essential duties.

The real threat to the horse cavalry began in October 1927, when Dwight Davis, secretary of war under President Coolidge, visited England. The English, struggling to avoid the static warfare of World War I, were testing a new concept: an independent force that included units of the combat arms—artillery, infantry and cavalry—and substituted motorized transportation for animal transportation as much as possible. It was called the Experimental Mechanized Force, and Secretary Davis saw it demonstrated on his visit.

Davis had combat experience (he was also the man who donated the Davis Cup to tennis after being half of the team that won the U.S. doubles championship three years in a row around 1900), and he liked what he saw. When he returned to the United States, he told the army chief of staff, General Charles P. Summerall, to establish a pilot program to test a U.S. Experimental Mechanized Force.

This force was to be composed of an infantry battalion transported in war-surplus trucks, a field artillery battalion with truck-transported guns, a cavalry armored car troop (even though the cavalry did not have an armored car troop), various support elements and the key component: two tank battalions and a tank platoon.

The new force was a definite break from previous U.S. Army organizations. The National Defense Act of 1920 had specifically confined tanks to the infantry. But tying tanks to infantry had slowed the development of tank tactics, and of tanks themselves, to the lumbering walk of an infantryman. A new dynamic was needed. So the commander of this new experimental force was not bound by the regulations of any one branch. He answered only to the War Department.

When units of the Experimental Mechanized Force began reporting to Camp Meade, Maryland, the first week of July 1928, most of the tanks were the same Renaults that the United States had used in World War I, only now older and even more prone to breakdowns.

The force's "armored cars" of the armored car troop were hastily assembled by Ordinance Corps personnel or troop mechanics at Camp Meade, who simply added boilerplate or light armor plates to the chassis of a Dodge, a La Salle and other cars that were handy. Armed with machine guns and equipped with radios, they were meant to be used for reconnaissance.

Not surprisingly, trial maneuvers of the force were unimpressive. Assigned new tasks for which it was not designed, the obsolete equipment broke down. Inadequate vehicles were used to test new theories of combined-arms employment. The force was dissolved after three months.

However, the War Office also had appointed a board to study mechanization. Despite the poor showing of the experimental force, on October 1, 1928, the board recommended establishment of a *permanent* mechanized force. Still, it was not until late 1930, when Davis no longer was secretary of war and Summerall was about to leave office, that Summerall actually ordered: "Assemble the mechanized force now....Make it permanent, not temporary."

But the force again was inadequate. Of the mere fifteen fighting tanks in the unit, all but three were the old 1917 model Renaults (although some had been modified with new engines). This force also was short-lived. The new army chief of staff, General Douglas MacArthur, dissolved it in May 1931. He had a different approach to mechanization, and it directly affected the cavalry.

CADETS GO MECHANIZED

In the meantime, the cadets at Fort Myer also experimented with mechanization beyond the scout car. They were quick to grasp the advantage of the car over the horse for their purpose—quick, long-distance transportation on weeknights and on weekends. From three-thirty until eleven o'clock each weekday, cadets were free to go wherever they wanted. On weekends, while one-third of the group had to stay to take care of the horses, two-thirds of the cadets were officially off from Saturday noon until reveille Monday morning.

Still, like the mechanized force, they, too, had problems due to old equipment. Charlie Wills, a VMI engineering cadet from Petersburg, Virginia, and a couple of buddies bought a 1925 Star touring car with a removable canvas top. About eleven o'clock one Sunday night, they started from Richmond, headed back to Fort Myer. Soon after leaving Richmond, they got partway up a long hill on Route 1 and the Star stalled. They got out, pushed it to the top of the hill and jumped in again as it rolled down the other side. They finally got it started on the way down, but the same thing happened at the next long hill. No amount of engineering expertise could keep it going. They performed this push-and-jump-in maneuver frequently until they arrived in camp an hour late and were rewarded with three weeks' confinement to post.

Then there was the 1923 Dodge that no driver could rely on: "You point it one way, by the time you got there, you had swerved somewhere else."

Charlie Dayhuff was driving his dilapidated Ford onto the post one afternoon with another cadet, Buddy Shell, the lanky son of an army officer from Fort Monroe, Virginia, when they saw Major Patton walking nearby. Patton was stationed across the Potomac River in Washington in the Office of the Chief of Cavalry, and that spring and summer of 1930, his articles warning of the danger of relying on mechanization had appeared in installments in the *Cavalry Journal*. Cadet Dayhuff had met Major Patton's older daughter, Bee, taken her out and gotten to know her father slightly.

Dayhuff stopped and politely asked Patton if he wanted a ride. As Dayhuff remembered years later, Patton's response was, "Ride that goddamn thing? If I was post commander, I wouldn't even allow it on post." This possibly was Patton's most succinct expression of his opinion of mechanization.

When, on weekends, the cadets were not riding their old cars off to faraway places, they sometimes attended weekend night dances at the Old Dominion Boat Club at the foot of King Street in nearby Alexandria. It was a good place to celebrate their temporary freedom from post. One night, however, a cadet celebrated too much, had too much to drink, passed out in the center of the street and ended up in the Alexandria jail.

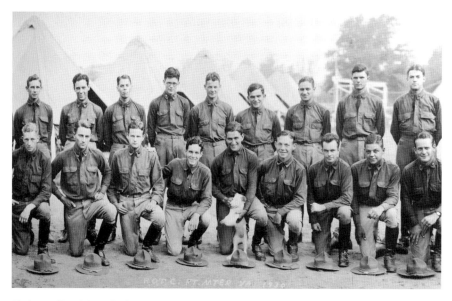

Cadets at Fort Myer. *Back row*: Pulliam (fifth from left), Shell (eighth from left). *Front row*: Roberts (middle, with the dog). *Author's collection.*

Early Old Dominion Boat Club. *Author's collection.*

Fortunately, when two other cadets came to the jail to get him out, the arresting officer was sympathetic. He told them that if they could get him sober, they could have him. Relieved, the cadets thought they had a chance to get him back to post before he, and they, would be missed.

They immediately went to their friend's cell, pulled him to his feet and got him walking, unsteadily, from one end of the cell to the other. Each time he passed one of his rescuers, he would receive a sound slap. Finally, just before dawn, the officer judged the incarcerated cadet was reasonably sober and set him free. All three cadets got back to the post just in time.

All the cadets' activity during weekdays and on weekends produced some very tired cavalrymen. A number of times, during the hot summer days, some cadets went off riding on assigned maneuvers while others waited their turn. One cadet remembered that the waiting men would stretch out on the ground, one after another, and quickly go to sleep holding their horses' reins. As a cadet slept, his horse wandered around and grazed, managing not to step on his rider or other cadets stretched out nearby.

During the next-to-last week of camp, the cadets traveled to a target range about twenty-five miles south of Fort Myer to qualify with their pistols. Instead of riding there on horseback, they drove their motley collection of twelve old cars.

In his Ford, Charlie Dayhuff led the convoy down the road in a single column. As they approached the range buildings, he signaled, and the cadet drivers fanned out impressively, part to the left and part to the right of him, just as on mounted maneuvers. Then all came to stop in a straight line in front of the main building. An old horse soldier standing nearby eyed the cars and asked one of their instructors, "What the hell are you doing teaching those kids those things? I thought you were a Cavalryman."

Tanks in the Stable Yard

It was a prophetic glimpse of things to come for the horse cavalry. New chief of staff Douglas MacArthur's idea for mechanization was to require all combat branches to mechanize, to the extent their budgets would allow. As part of this plan, on May 1, 1931, he ordered parts of the newly reformed "permanent" mechanized force, including some tanks, to be subsumed into the cavalry as a reinforced regiment. Shortly afterward, he also ordered two cavalry regiments to turn in their horses for tanks.

Yet the old National Defense Act of 1920 still provided that only the infantry was to have tanks. MacArthur got around it by referring to the tanks sent to the cavalry as "combat cars." (With this subterfuge, he was carrying on something of a tradition—the use of the term *tank* evolved originally when the first of those vehicles was sent from Britain to France during World War I under tight security in crates labeled "desert water carrier.")

The cavalry now was forced to deal directly with tanks. As an article in the *Louisville Courier Journal* reported soon after the order: "'Boots and saddles' now means 'crank 'er up.'"

MacArthur's action reflected the two schools of thought about horse versus machine that had existed in the cavalry for several years. To some it seemed obvious that improved machines could perform all the traditional cavalry functions better than horses. Others—and in the 1920s, they were the ones in control of the cavalry— firmly believed that the horse could not be replaced. Major Patton and like thinkers were in this latter group. They maintained that the horse had to remain the focus of the cavalry—only the horse had the ability to perform all cavalry functions in all weather and all terrains. Patton went even further: "When Sampson took the fresh jawbone of an ass and slew a thousand men therewith he probably started such a vogue for the weapon, especially among the Philistines, that for years no prudent donkey dared to bray….Today machines hold the place formerly occupied by the jawbone….They too shall pass."

Yet a smoke-belching tank reeking of oil had rumbled into the stable yard, parked and now stood there among the bags of oats, showing every intention of staying. And it was disturbing the horses.

In an attempt to reassure the horse advocates, the then chief of cavalry sought a middle ground: "[I]n the future we will have two types of cavalry, one with armored motor vehicles giving speed, strategical mobility and great fighting power of modern machines; the other with horses, armed with the latest automatic firearms for use in tactical roles and for operations in difficult terrain where the horse still gives us the greatest mobility."

Meanwhile, the War Department proceeded to organize the new mechanized cavalry unit. It chose Fort Knox, Kentucky, for its station and designated it the Seventh Cavalry Brigade (Mechanized).

This new unit was placed under the command of the V Army Corps area commander. The chief of cavalry's role was limited to making recommendations and conducting inspections, the latter only under War Department direction.

In 1933, the First Cavalry was moved to Fort Knox from Marfa, Texas, and became the first cavalry unit to give up its horses for combat cars. But political pressure from local jurisdictions that would lose their cavalry regiments kept a second regiment from surrendering its horses and moving to Fort Knox until 1936. Then the Thirteenth Cavalry was moved from the Cavalry School at Fort Riley, Kansas, to join the Seventh Cavalry Brigade at Fort Knox.

At its other posts, the horse cavalry continued to train for its mission while nervously looking out of the corner of its eye at the tank revving its engines in the stable yard.

More and more, the horse seemed an anachronism, yet it was an alluring anachronism. And this allure had always been a factor in its survival. For others, there was the history: knights in armor, J.E.B. Stuart and Phil Sheridan, the old Indian fighters, Teddy Roosevelt and the Rough Riders. Then the sports: polo, fox hunting, jumping. "If any branch of the Old Army evoked romance," wrote historian Edward M. Coffman recently in his foreword to *The Twilight of the U.S. Cavalry* by General Lucian K. Truscott Jr., "it was the pageantry of cavalry, with the military horsemen in full panoply, the chattering bugles, and snapping red and white guidons." All these factors helped the horse cavalry survive deep into the 1930s.

A story making the rounds of the cavalry posts then, from Fort Myer to Fort Meade, South Dakota, told of a brigadier in the British army who asked a lieutenant of the horse cavalry: "What is the value of the Launcers in the present-day Army?" The lieutenant hesitated, but the brigadier insisted, "Come, come now, Leftenant. What is the value of the Launcers in modern warfare?" The lieutenant finally replied, "Well, my Lord, you must admit that the Launcers add a bit of tone to what would otherwise be a very vulgar sort of a brawl."

But the dashing history, parades and pageantry were being scrutinized by colder and colder eyes. In 1938, as World War II approached, two hard-driving men were appointed to important cavalry commands, and they went head-to-head over horse versus machine. Major General John K. Herr was appointed chief of cavalry, and Brigadier General Adna R. Chaffee was appointed commander of the Seventh Cavalry Brigade (Mechanized). They fought to the finish, with only one command left standing at the end.

Both were cavalry officers who, early in their careers, had distinguished themselves as excellent riders. Herr was one of the army's best polo players, a member of the legendary 1923 U.S. team that defeated a strongly favored British team. Chaffee was the youngest member of the 1911 U.S. team in

Regular army rider jumps his horse over a dinner table. *Library of Congress.*

the International Horse Show in London during George V's coronation week and a former student at the French Cavalry School at Saumur, France (where he learned to jump over fully set dinner tables without overturning a glass of water).

Both were graduates of the United States Military Academy. Both had served in World War I as staff officers—Herr as the chief of staff of the Thirtieth Infantry Division ("Old Hickory") and Chaffee on the general staff at the headquarters of the American Expeditionary Force.

A major difference, however, was that Chaffee was in General Summerall's Operations and Training Section, G-3, in 1927 when Secretary Davis and Summerall began what was to be the modern tank corps. At that point, Chaffee had never ridden in a tank, but the more he learned about tanks, the more interested he became. On the other hand, when Herr was appointed in 1938, he had no known sympathy for tanks and had just spent the previous two and a half years commanding the legendary Indian fighters, the Seventh Cavalry, at Fort Bliss, Texas.

Herr soon made his point of view known. In congressional testimony in 1939, he stated that the cavalry must "maintain a proper balance between horse and mechanized units" in order to maintain maximum efficiency.

Mechanized vehicles were "unable, even though moving across country, to negotiate the many difficult types of terrain such as woods, bogs, streams, stone walls, and ditches which are easy for the horse." The number of mechanized units in the cavalry could increase, but no man on horse would be given up to organize these new units. As he expressed it, "We must not be misled to our own detriment to assume that the untried machine can displace the proved and tried horse."

Chaffee, on the other hand, was trying to increase the size of his "combat car" brigade and form a full division. At first, Chaffee thought he had Herr's support. But time passed, and the plans for the expansion lay quietly on some War Office desk. When he read Herr's public comments, he realized no support would be forthcoming from that direction. He must turn elsewhere.

In April 1939, word arrived that General George C. Marshall (a VMI graduate) would soon be appointed chief of staff. Marshall was less attached to set army practices than previous chiefs of staff. Shortly afterward, Chaffee persuaded Marshall to listen to his views. He found Marshall open to expanding the mechanized brigade but still unconvinced.

WORLD WAR II BEGINS

That was how things stood in September 1939 when the German blitzkrieg struck Poland. Only a few months earlier, the *Cavalry Journal* had carried articles noting Poland's large commitment to cavalry and explaining how Poland planned to use it, with the unspoken message that here was an admirable European nation that still believed strongly in the value of its horses in modern war. Then the Germans attacked Poland from the north, west and south. Massed columns of German tanks, backed by waves of dive bombers and followed by mechanized infantry, pouring through gaps created by other tanks and planes, found the Polish cavalry completely inadequate.

General Chaffee delivered a lecture at the Army War College only a few weeks after the invasion of Poland. He discussed in some detail the success of the blitzkrieg. He concluded: "There is no longer any shadow of a doubt as to the efficiency of well trained and boldly led mechanized forces in any war of movement [and] that they cannot be combated by infantry and horse cavalry alone." He further recommended the establishment in the near future of at least four mechanized cavalry divisions.

Polish cavalry, 1939. *Wikimedia Commons.*

Herr continued to oppose expanding the Seventh Brigade at the expense of horse cavalry, but the War Department was beginning to grow tired of his intransigence. General Marshall ordered wargame maneuvers to be held April 12–25 and May 5–25, 1940, in Georgia and Louisiana, and for the first time, a mechanized unit larger than a brigade was to be employed by combining Chaffee's combat cars with some infantry tanks.

Several months before the maneuvers, Patton, now a colonel and commander of the horse cavalry at Fort Myer, slipped inside information about the general maneuver scenario and the cavalry's particular mission to the head of the horse cavalry arm in the maneuvers, his friend Major General Kenyon Joyce. Patton, who had been uncharacteristically silent for a while, also managed to get himself appointed an umpire for the maneuvers so he could observe firsthand what happened.

What happened was that Joyce's horses were unable to keep pace with Chaffee's combat cars, particularly during the fourth phase of the maneuvers. In that phase, the great majority of the tanks were on the side of the red army, while the horses were with the blue. Red, spearheaded by Chaffee's tanks, swept around to attack blue's flanks. Blue's horses rushed to stop them, but the red tanks consistently beat the horses to vital unguarded road junctions and other crucial sites. They then defended these sites long enough for red's line troops, following behind the tanks, to establish positions that critically endangered the blue army. Even with Patton's inside information, the horse cavalry could not contain the mechanized forces.

That same May, German panzers moved quickly into Holland, Belgium and France.

On the last day of maneuvers, May 25, 1940, an impromptu conference on mechanization was held in the basement of the Alexandria, Louisiana high school. Present were General Chaffee, General Frank Andrews of the War Department general staff (Marshall's man) and a few others, including, somehow, Colonel Patton. Not included was General Herr, although he was in Louisiana at the same time. Those present concluded unanimously "that development of mechanized units could no longer be delayed, and that such units must be removed from the control of the traditional branch to become a separate organization," as Mildred H. Gillie reports in her book *Forging the Thunderbolt.* On July 10, 1940, General Marshall issued the order creating an armored force. General Chaffee was appointed its first commander.

The days of the horse cavalry were numbered. It lasted until March 9, 1942, when the office of chief of cavalry was eliminated and its functions were transferred to the newly formed army ground forces. General Herr retired from active duty a few days before the transfer. But by then, the meeting-and-memo war was over, and the real war for the United States had begun. None of the ten remaining horse cavalry regiments went overseas to World War II with their horses.

Philippines: Horses Meet Tanks

One regiment of the U.S. cavalry, however, did meet the enemy with its horses. Its horses already were overseas, and the enemy—with tanks—came to meet them.

On December 22, 1941, the Japanese landed on Luzon Island in the Philippines, approximately one hundred miles north of the head of Manila Bay. Quickly, it became apparent that the strength of the Japanese force and the lack of training of the Philippine army meant that the most the United States could expect early on was to delay the enemy from its drive south toward Manila.

One of the best trained U.S. units in the Philippines was the Twenty-Sixth Cavalry Regiment (Philippine Scouts). This horse cavalry unit, organized in 1922, was composed of handpicked Filipino NCOs and men led by American officers.

The Twenty-Sixth, fighting dismounted along with other U.S. units, met the enemy within sight of the beach, but it was hit with infantry, tanks, planes and naval bombardment and forced to withdraw to a second position.

Here occurred the first contact between U.S. mounted troops and enemy tanks. Although the engagement began almost humorously, it ended in near disaster.

In the withdrawal, the U.S. forces had broken off contact with the Japanese. After setting up its second position, the Twenty-Sixth was ordered to move back again to still another new position. It was night when they received the order, and the regiment was strung out along either side of a paved road. As the regiment was preparing to mount up and leave, several U.S. light tanks that had been up ahead motored through the ranks of the Twenty-Sixth and on back down the road.

Next, Captain John Wheeler, commander of Troop E, saw two more tanks clank up the middle of the road toward the regiment and stop. He rode toward these newcomers and yelled for them to get moving. A turret on one opened, a head popped up, Captain Wheeler let out a few colorful words, the head popped back down and the turret closed. Then the Japanese tank opened fire.

Suddenly, several Japanese tanks were in the midst of the Twenty-Sixth firing their guns, catching some troopers up on their horses, others still on the ground. High banks topped by fences lined each side of the dark road, leaving the cavalrymen little room to deploy. Horses bucked and reared. Mounted troops ran into dismounted. As one officer tried to mount, his horse bolted, catching his foot in the stirrup, dragging him along the road and knocking him unconscious. Several troopers were trampled by terrified horses. Mounted men and riderless horses ran down the road in complete confusion.

Captain Wheeler and Major Thomas J.H. Trapnell were bringing up the rear of the rush of horsemen when they came to a bridge. Just then, on the other side of the bridge, the regimental veterinarian truck drove up. Wheeler and Trapnell dashed across the bridge to the truck, and under heavy machine gun fire from the pursuing Japanese tanks, they and the vet pushed the truck onto the middle of the bridge and set it on fire.

This act stopped the Japanese tanks on the far side of the bridge, and the Twenty-Sixth was able to restore order within its ranks. But this fight had been a defeat, as the cavalry's first encounter with the machine gun twenty-three years earlier had been a defeat.

As the Japanese continued their advance south, the Twenty-Sixth fought courageously and fell back and fought and fell back again down Luzon Island.

About three weeks after the Japanese landing, in a small village of thatched-roofed grass huts on the west coast of Luzon, the Twenty-Sixth executed the U.S. Army's last horse cavalry charge. It was a mad dash by a little over twenty troopers plunging their horses forward, their pistols flashing, into the startled faces of an advance unit of Japanese infantry. The charge halted the Japanese advance, but only briefly. Even with the subsequent aid of a full division of Filipino troops, the action only bought a twenty-four-hour delay in the steady Japanese advance down Luzon and onto the Bataan Peninsula.

The same Captain Wheeler who had met the tanks was the commander of the Twenty-Sixth's forces at the village when the cavalry charged. He was wounded in the leg. Later, he was captured when the U.S. forces surrendered at Bataan, and he died in captivity.

Other U.S. cavalry units were more successful fighting as armored units in World War II, and a number of individual cavalrymen played vital roles in the U.S. victory in the war. Ernest N. Harmon, who wrote about the cavalry's unfortunate experiences in World War I, commanded armored divisions in North Africa, Italy, Belgium and Germany. Lucian K. Truscott Jr., a tough polo player who was commissioned in the cavalry in 1917, commanded the Third Infantry Division in Sicily, the VI Corps at Anzio and during the invasion of southern France and the Fifth Army in Italy. And, of course, giving invaluable aid to the victory was George S. Patton Jr. and his tanks.

CADETS GO TO WAR

Almost none of the ROTC cadet-trainees went into the military directly after graduation in 1931—the United States wanted a small standing army then. However, they served in a surprisingly wide variety of capacities during the war.

Charlie Wills, part owner of the Star automobile, somehow got into the navy and served as an engineering officer on a destroyer escorting convoys across the North Atlantic. Charlie Dayhuff was in military intelligence, stationed in Brazil, searching for German submarine hideouts and monitoring suspected raw rubber smuggling. His lanky friend Buddy Shell became a marine and was severely wounded when a Japanese shell landed at his artillery command post just inland from the beach during the second day of the invasion of Saipan. He survived to become a lieutenant general and superintendent at VMI.

Eddie Pulliam, of the one-eyed horse, trained with barrage balloons—large, thick-skinned, dirigible-shaped balloons sent aloft over U.S. and English cities to deter low-flying enemy aircraft. He ended up as the executive officer of a mobile replacement station that moved across the French countryside housing and feeding troops on their way to the front lines.

Louie Roberts, of the small black horse, was one of the few to serve with the horse cavalry's old nemesis—tanks. Shortly before the Normandy invasion, he and a British tank officer were ordered to swap places. Roberts became the commander of a British tank squadron training in England with experimental tanks and told of accompanying the unit in the invasion. Later, after MacArthur's return to the Philippines, he led U.S. tanks against the Japanese.

There still are horses at Fort Myer. The low, red-brick stables stand today where they did in the summer of 1930, and before that. Some shelter horses whose duty is to accompany funerals in nearby Arlington National Cemetery, where so many cavalrymen now rest.

These horses continue to be cared for by young troopers, who must groom them carefully after the horses' duties are over, and before they themselves are allowed to do anything else.

NOTE: WHEN THIS ARTICLE was first published in May 2002, the cavalry charge in the Philippines in 1941 certainly appeared to have been the U.S. Army's last horse cavalry charge. And it was, in the sense that it was done by an organized unit of the U.S. Army composed of Filipino regulars trained and led by U.S. Army officers.

Sixty years later, however, on October 23, 2001, two members of the U.S. Army's Special Forces, Captain Mitch Nelson and Staff Sergeant Charles Jones, wearing tan camouflage fatigues, and three CIA paramilitary officers, Mike Spann, Dave Olson and J.J. Sawyer, wearing jeans and hiking boots from L.L. Bean, participated in a charge on horseback in Afghanistan against the Taliban as part of a unit of Afghan fighters led by an Afghan general, Abdul Rashid Dostum.

They attacked about one thousand Taliban fighters who were dug into trenches and armed with shoulder-fired rocket-propelled grenades, AK-47s and mortars and supported by three tanks and two ZSU-23s—self-propelled, tracked, low-altitude antiaircraft fighting vehicles armed with four 23mm

United States Army Special Forces in tan camouflage fatigues ride with Afghans in 2001: Afghans in front, Special Forces horsemen spread out behind. *Wikimedia Commons/Master Sergeant Chris Spence.*

cannons that could be directed at infantry as well as aircraft—all about half a mile away over several hills and an open plain. The Afghans had about six hundred men on horses and on foot, plus the five Americans. According to Doug Stanton's book *Horse Soldiers*, their battle plan was that "the horsemen would charge the middle, the infantry would attack the flanks, and machine guns set on adjoining hills would spray covering fire."

Just as the horsemen began their charge, bombs dropped from a jet overhead called in by Captain Nelson exploded on the Taliban line, hitting close to the tanks, destroying a ZSU-23, demoralizing the Taliban and exciting the surging Afghans.

The rest of the battle was not easy, but the Taliban soon fled for their lives. The international combination of a jet, machine gunners, infantry *and* horse soldiers had won.

Chapter 10

SHIPBUILDERS, GUNRUNNERS AND DUELISTS

Robinson Landing, 1749–2007

If you stand at the intersection of Union and Duke Streets today and look around, what you see is very different from what you would have seen on that same spot in early 1749, before there was a Duke or a Union Street and before there was even an Alexandria.

Moreover, had you returned to that spot from time to time during the intervening years, not only would you have seen changes, but you also would have met a variety of singular people. This chapter describes some of those changes and tells the stories of some of those people—shipbuilders and factory builders, seamen and duelists and even gunrunners.

THE LAND

This chapter was first published as an article in the 2007 issue of the *Alexandria Chronicle*. If you had walked to the foot of Duke Street then, and many years before that, only a small park would have separated you from the Potomac River to the east. Looking north, up the Strand toward Washington, you would have seen, on the street's right side, three worn, bedraggled buildings used for storage and repair of small boats and on the left, a long, red-brick warehouse containing part of the Art League School. To the south, toward Mount Vernon, would have been the office building, large warehouses and dock of the Robinson Terminal Warehouse Corporation. To the west, Duke Street crossed Union Street, as it does today.

Robinson Terminal South at the foot of Duke Street, 2007. *Author's collection.*

Until 1749, Alexandria did not exist. There were no streets and no buildings. Instead, about sixty feet east (toward the river) from where Union Street is today stood an earthen bank about fifteen to twenty feet high (roughly level with present-day Lee Street). From this height, the bank fell steeply to dry ground, which stretched farther east from the bank's foot until it ended in a rounded point with the river lapping on both its sides and flowing by its end. This point was named Point Lumley after a Captain Lumley who once moored his ship just offshore.

Going north on the river from Point Lumley, the high bank curved gradually inland and then gradually out again to another point at the end of present-day Oronoco Street. At the foot of this curved bank washed a shallow, crescent-shaped bay. Along the bank's top were built the first streets, houses and stores of Alexandria.

COLONIAL PERIOD

In 1749, most of the undeveloped lots in Alexandria were sold to private investors; however, the Alexandria town trustees retained Point Lumley to be used for public purposes.

155

Two years later, the trustees cut Duke Street through the high bank to open up the point for business. At roughly the same time, they leased Point Lumley to Thomas Fleming, a young ship's carpenter from Annapolis.

Fleming saw a future for himself in the new town. He saw a seaport in need of ships but without a shipyard to build them. Thus, he began constructing a few buildings on the point to help with his new shipbuilding operations—probably walls around a large pit and a roof over it to protect men working on a hull inside from the weather, a tool shed and some small support buildings. (These were the first of many buildings constructed on and around the point.) By 1752, he had finished his first ship, the *Ranger*,

Opposite: Point Lumley, circa 1760. *Alexandria Archaeology*.

Above: Alexandria's crescent-shaped harbor overlaid on modern streets. *Alexandria Archaeology*.

a 154-ton, eight-gun ship manned by a crew of twelve, built for a trading company from Whitehaven, England.

Thomas Fleming prospered. In 1763, he bought the lot on the river just south of Point Lumley and began "banking out." He first constructed a coffer dam, whose wooden walls held back water from an area of the river bottom adjoining his new lot. He then leveled the lot's bank and piled the dirt and stones removed from the bank on the cleared river bottom inside the dam and sometimes into wooden structures, such as the hull of an old sailing ship, placed on the cleared bottom. Continuing in this way, he gradually made new land and constructed a wharf on some of it. (Years later, in 2018, parts of the hulls of three ships were discovered in land near Point Lumley that had been banked out.)

The same year, 1763, Fleming was appointed a town trustee. In 1770, he bought the lot adjoining Point Lumley to the west and conveyed his old lot to his son-in-law, keeping it in the family.

Soon afterward, however, Fleming's shipbuilding operation faltered, then failed. In 1771, Alexandria merchant Harry Piper wrote, "I believe Ship building is done at Alexandria, as there is no Timber to be got." In 1774, Piper wrote again, "We have no Vessels a building, nor likely to have any."

Revolutionary Era

During the American Revolution and shortly afterward, the banking out process extended Point Lumley and created an area of wharves and useful land adjoining the point to the south, between Duke and Wolfe Streets. As the banks were leveled, the character of the area began to change.

In 1780, Alexandria trustees leased property on the point to Robert Townshend Hooe and Richard Harrison, who soon built a warehouse of stone and wood on the wharf there and established the very successful commission merchant firm of Hooe and Harrison. That same year, Hooe became the town's first elected mayor. He was also a militia colonel during the Revolutionary War and later, a friend of George Washington's who dined often at Mount Vernon.

Hooe and Harrison were cousins, and they first began working together in the very early days of the Revolutionary War. In fact, their efforts contributed to the success of the American patriots.

At the start of the Revolution in June 1775, Lord Dunmore, the royal governor of Virginia, had been forced to flee Williamsburg in a British man-of-war. Directing the ship, Dunmore captured Norfolk and began to harass shipping along the Chesapeake Bay and raid rebel homes. Understandably, the revolutionaries in Baltimore and Alexandria feared for their safety, in part because they knew they were unable to defend themselves—they lacked the basic military supplies of gunpowder and muskets.

At that time, Robert Townshend Hooe was part of the firm of Jenifer and Hooe. The Jenifer of the firm lived in Port Tobacco, Maryland, and was chairman of the important Maryland Council of Safety.

Attempting to obtain material to defend the colony, at the end of 1775 and in early 1776, the Maryland Council of Safety dispatched several ships to the then neutral French island of Martinique. Because the French and British were not then at war with each other, French ships could come and go from the island carrying gunpowder and other military supplies without being seized by the British. The colonists soon realized that, at Martinique, they could pick up supplies more easily than by sailing to France and risking confrontation with the numerous ships of the British navy.

The council's plan was to sell goods from their ships in Martinique, use the funds received to buy gunpowder, muskets and other supplies from the French and then return home without being intercepted by the English. To handle transactions in Martinique between Maryland and the French, the council dispatched the young Baltimore merchant Richard Harrison.

Robert Townshend Hooe in Alexandria, working with Jenifer and the Maryland council, began corresponding with Harrison in Martinique. On the council's behalf, Hooe bought a ship and loaded it with goods for Martinique and procured goods for two other ships bound for the island, including one owned by his own firm.

The ships' chances of arriving in Martinique and returning safely, however, still were not good. An American merchant wrote to the Maryland Council of Safety that the British were seizing a number of American vessels in the West Indies, and "I tremble for such vessels as is destined for St. Eustia and Martinico."

One of Hooe's three ships arrived safely in Martinique and returned with valuable supplies. A second, however, was chased by a British warship into port on the island. There, after unloading it, Harrison reloaded it with gunpowder, cleverly camouflaged the ship's ownership and destination, put on board several Frenchmen to pose as crew and sent it out again. Fortunately, the ship made it back safely to the Potomac; some of its powder made its way to Alexandria. The third ship, unfortunately, was captured by the British, taken into Martinique and sold as a prize. But the creative Harrison arranged for a Frenchman to buy it, load it with gunpowder and sail it back home. This time, it arrived safely in the Potomac.

This flagrant American activity caused the British authorities to complain to the French governor of Martinique and to single out Harrison as the American head conspirator. However, even though the French were not at war with the English, they were finding the war between the English and the Americans profitable

Hooe and Harrifon,
Have for Sale at their Store,

OSnaburgs, Ravens duck, brown rolls, Ruffia duck, Holland's ditto, white-lead, red ditto, Spanifh brown, red ochre, yellow ditto, white vitriol, verdigreafe, brimftone, fand-glaffes, fpy-glaffes, fheet-lead, fheet-copper, German fteel, loglines, deepfea ditto, houfeline, marline, hamberline, fail twine, feine ditto, fheet-tin in boxes, fteel wire, tar, turpentine, Englifh and Dutch cordage, anchors of different fizes, mould candles, Hyfon, bohea and fouchong tea, black pepper, fingle refined and double refined fugar, candied ditto, gin in cafes, mufkets, butter pots, water pitchers, queen's china, glafs ware, delf bowls, long and fhort pipes, violins, looking-glaffes, hatchets, carpenters' and joiners' tools, fcythes, bolting-cloths, blankets, flannels, hats, cotton ftockings, yarn and worfted ditto, diaper napkins, cambricks, lawns, check fhirts, gauze handkerchiefs, old hock in bottles, &c.
Alexandria, Jan. 26, 1785.

Hooe and Harrison advertisement. *Alexandria Gazette, February 3, 1785.*

both politically and commercially. The French governor blithely wrote back denying that arms or powder "for the rebellious subjects of His Britannic Majesty" had been procured as alleged. Moreover, he wrote that Richard Harrison, instead of being some sort of American agent, was in fact but "a young man of 20 [he actually was 26], come in the ship *Baltimore*, to St. Pierre [in Martinique] in order to be treated for venereal disease." Hooe and Harrison continued their activities.

Later in the Revolutionary War, Harrison became the acting consul representing America in Cádiz, Spain. Thus, he developed, through his wartime experience, connections with Alexandria's two major foreign trading areas at that time, the West Indies and Europe.

Harrison and Hooe impressed each other and, toward the end of the war, entered into a partnership that continued well into the 1790s. From their wharf just south of Duke Street, the shipping firm of Hooe and Harrison would take orders from abroad, or from coastal American cities, for Alexandria's main export commodities—wheat, flour, Indian corn and tobacco. To fill the orders, the firm would buy flour, for example, transported into Alexandria by wagons from Loudon County and other backcountry areas and pay for it, and for their commission, by drawing on funds the firms placing the orders deposited in banks in England or maybe Philadelphia. They then would load the goods onto tall sailing ships at their wharf and send them on to their destinations.

At times, ships would arrive in Alexandria with goods to sell, and then Hooe and Harrison would act as the ships' agents, selling the cargo—anything from muskets and anchors to violins, flutes, hand mirrors, Spanish wines and rich cloth—and taking their commissions from the proceeds.

While this type of shipping activity was taking place on the wharves located between Duke and Wolfe Streets, the part of the block away from the water's edge was crowded with businesses that supported shipping, including a ship chandler, a barrel maker and a ship's biscuit baker. People lived above some of these establishments, and others, including free African Americans, filled several tenements nearby. At one time, this part of the block was divided into as many as twenty-two separate parcels.

Between 1782 and 1785, a new street, Union Street, was cut through the block on its western side. As the banking out process proceeded, in 1802, the street called the Strand was continued south across Duke Street and on through the block to connect Duke and Wolfe Streets.

In 1809, R.T. Hooe died. He had been a hardnosed businessman who, not long before his death, wrote an unusual will. In it, he said he was making a will because if he did not, he was afraid his property would go to "what in Law is called an 'Heir.'" He was concerned that this "Heir" might be

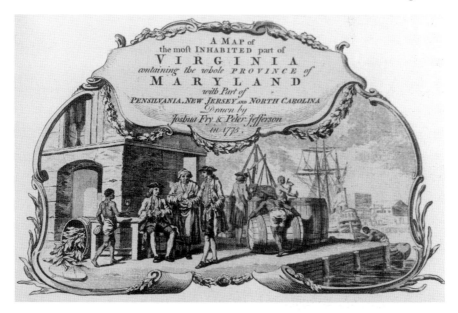

Conducting business as was done at the foot of Duke Street: from the Fry-Jefferson map, 1751. *Library of Congress.*

"a person whom I, in my life time disliked, and would as soon have given anything to a puppy." He then listed those types of undesirable persons: "The Card Player, the horse racer, The Beau, The Fop, are among others, the Beings in human shape, whom I detest, and look upon as a Pest to Society, and as such ought to be driven from among the honest part of Mankind."

Corsairs

Harrison, after forming the partnership with Hooe, continued to live abroad. In 1784, he was still acting American consul in Cádiz, as well as being a private merchant, when an incident involving him and a ship from Alexandria led to the first treaty between the United States and a Muslim country.

The treaty came about as follows. In October 1784, the brig *Betsy* from Alexandria docked in Cádiz. After the crew unloaded merchandise for Consul Harrison, they refilled the *Betsy*'s hold with salt and dry goods and set sail for Tenerife in the Canary Islands. On board as second mate was the consul's twenty-three-year-old nephew and namesake, Richard Harrison. Later, the nephew related in a deposition what happened next.

The *Betsy* had not sailed far out into the Atlantic when her crew saw a ship approaching. It looked like the English ship that had docked near them in

Barbary Coast corsair. *Penterest.*

Cádiz. Only when the ship got closer could they see that the crew wore the turbans of the dreaded Barbary pirates. By then, it was too late. The corsairs captured the *Betsy* and took her to their home port: Tangier, Morocco.

All was not lost, however. Morocco's sultan, Sidi Muhammad, desired a treaty with the United States. (Seven years earlier, in 1777, the sultan had been the first head of state to formally recognize America's independence.) Capture of the *Betsy* was his way of getting the new nation's attention. As an indication of his goodwill, the sultan treated the captive seamen well and less than a year after their capture, returned them, including the consul's nephew, to Harrison in Cádiz. In 1787, negotiations between the United States and Morocco produced a treaty regularizing relations between the two countries.

The older Richard Harrison eventually settled in Alexandria and married the daughter of George Washington's physician and friend James Craik. Shortly after Harrison's term as consul, John Adams referred to him favorably as "a Gentleman of much Merit." Later, President George Washington appointed Harrison auditor of the treasury, a position he held for forty-five years until his death in 1841 at the age of ninety-two.

MID-NINETEENTH CENTURY

Just before the Civil War, the waterfront block between Duke and Wolfe Streets began to take on a more industrial character. By 1851, railroad tracks had been laid down Union Street from the Wilkes Street tunnel to Oronoco Street, separating the block from the rest of Alexandria and intensifying its industrial feel.

In 1853, two Alexandrians, William H. Fowle and his younger brother George, teamed with several New York City investors to lease much of the block for ninety-nine years to build a steam-driven flour plant called Pioneer Mill. It was finished in 1854 and at six stories high was one of the largest such plants in the United States and one of the tallest buildings in Alexandria. It could take wheat straight off the dock into the plant and there mill the wheat into flour at a rate of up to eight hundred barrels a day. Most of that flour was sold to businesses in New York.

Willian H. Fowle, the chief operating officer of the company, was literally a marked man. Twenty-five years earlier, his face had been badly disfigured in a duel fought with another Alexandrian, Lewis A. Cazenove.

In 1827, when both Fowle and Cazenove were in their twenties, there was a fire at a local business called Ladd's Mill. Cazenove wrote to his brother in Boston describing the fire and said that he had seen William H. Fowle and his father standing by while neighbors fought the fire to keep it from destroying the mill. Even worse, he added that the Fowles were seen "looking on with apparent self-satisfaction."

This story circulated in Boston, where the Fowles had connections, and made its way back to Alexandria. The Fowles were infuriated, and the younger William H. tried to get Cazenove to retract his statements. Cazenove did retract them to some extent, but not enough to satisfy Fowle. To preserve the family honor, Fowle challenged Cazenove to a duel. Seconds were appointed, pistols chosen and a date and place set for the confrontation: December 26, the day after Christmas, across the river in Maryland.

Fowle was a militia officer and had some familiarity with weapons, but Cazenove, according to a letter written by his father just after the duel, had never held a loaded pistol in his hand until late the night before the duel, when someone convinced him to do some practicing.

At the appointed time, the two squared off and fired. Each side's witnesses said that their man fired first. Nevertheless, Fowle's bullet completely missed, while Cazenove's hit Fowle in the face.

For a few days, there was doubt whether Fowle would survive. He did, but his face was badly disfigured. As for Lewis Cazenove, a friend wrote to his father, "There is no harm in being thought a great shot provided it does not become a habit, and I strongly advise Lewis to let it rest there, if only that he may not injure his reputation by a bad shot."

Both men continued to live in Alexandria. Inevitably, from time to time, they must have met each other walking along a street.

Civil War

Later in life, William H. Fowle was more successful, becoming a director in the Orange and Alexandria Railroad, president of the Chesapeake and Ohio Canal Company and president of the Bank of Old Dominion. However, he was as unlucky in the flour business as in dueling. His company's flour plant, Pioneer Mill, located on the river between Duke and Wolfe Streets, was reasonably successful for seven years, from 1854 until

Pioneer Mill. *Alexandria Library/Special Collections, VF-Civil War Collection.*

1861. In 1861, however, when the Civil War began in Alexandria, Union forces took control of Alexandria and turned the mill into a warehouse for army commissary goods.

In addition, President Lincoln blockaded Alexandria from commercial imports and exports as part of his blockade of all southern ports, although he permitted military goods to be imported on behalf of the Union. The blockade of Alexandria was not lifted until September 1863, after the battle of Gettysburg and after Alexandria became the capital of the Restored Government of Virginia, which consisted of the part of Virginia controlled by the Union. Apparently, Alexandria was then considered safely under Union control.

LATE NINETEENTH CENTURY

Alexandria was slow to recover from the Civil War. In 1869, the city council was unable to pay principal and interests on its bonds. As a result, to secure payment to its creditors, the city turned over to trustees much of its real property, some of its personal property and all rents from leases of that property. Included in the transfer were the jail, Market Square and the fire department buildings, as well as the department's horses, horse harnesses and fire engines. It also included Point Lumley. Over the following years, however, the property in trust was either sold or returned to Alexandria.

The Duke-to-Wolfe-Streets block was part of this slow recovery. If a person owned property on the block before the Civil War, almost without exception, that person or the person's heirs owned the property until the 1870s or later. In 1875, Pioneer Mill was finally sold at a fraction of its original cost.

The block was to suffer a further setback. In the early morning dark of June 3, 1897, a fire started in the block just north of Duke Street and spread to the Pioneer Mill, with devastating results. When light came later that day, all that was left of the towering, long-standing Alexandria landmark, according to the *Alexandria Gazette*, was "a mass of smoldering ruins."

EARLY TWENTIETH CENTURY

During the early part of the twentieth century, the block began a slow comeback. It was used for light industrial activities, such as an oil storage facility, a railroad freight depot, a lumberyard, a secondhand machinery sales and repair shop and a small automobile production plant. In 1906, one of the first automobiles built in Virginia was assembled on this block by the Emerson Engine Company.

In 1939, much of the block was bought by the Robinson Terminal Warehouse Corporation, a company that specialized in storing and shipping newsprint and copy paper for newspapers. Until the early 1970s, the corporation also unloaded small arms from ships for Interarms, a neighboring gun merchant on Union Street—once again, the block dealt in firearms. In 1982, the Warehouse Corporation was sold to the Washington Post Company.

At the height of its shipping activity in the early 1980s, sixty freighters a year unloaded goods at the terminal on Duke Street or the one on Oronoco Street. By contrast, only one freighter docked at the facility in 2002.

Ship unloading cargo at foot of Duke Street. *Alexandria Library/Special Collections, VF-Waterfront Collection.*

2007

Today, the Washington Post still operates the Warehouse Corporation. It occupies the entire block and still deals primarily in paper products—newsprint, copy paper and "food grade paper"—the kind of paper used to wrap McDonald's hamburgers and Kentucky Fried Chicken. Parts of its Duke Street facility also are used by a local man to repair racing sculls for area rowing teams and by the Alexandria Seaport Foundation for its boat-building program.

The facility in the block between Duke and Wolfe consists of six buildings: three warehouses, a building for storing and repairing forklifts and trucks, a small equipment storage building and an office building. Although some of the warehouses may contain parts of earlier buildings, for the most part, the buildings you see today were built in the twentieth century.

The office building at 2 Duke Street, however, may be more than one hundred years old, although its façade is much newer. It stands roughly

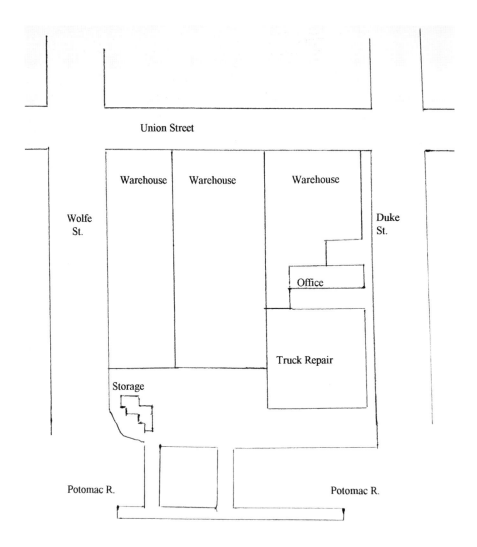

Map of Robinson Terminal South, 2007. *Author's collection.*

where the old Hooe and Harrison stone warehouse stood but seems not to be the same size, in precisely the same location or of the same material as the earlier building. However, a building the same size as the current building is shown on the 1877 Hopkins map of Alexandria and on an even earlier Civil War map. On the latter, its use is indicated as a "Soldiers Messhouse."

It would be surprising if the office building actually survived the 1897 fire that destroyed Pioneer Mill, then located not far away to the east, toward

Robinson Terminal South Office Building, 2007. *Author's collection.*

the river. However, Willie Taylor, operations manager of the Robinson Terminal Warehouse Corporation, said in the summer of 2006 that several years earlier, he had been in the office building's attic and seen scorched beams in the northeast corner of the attic's ceiling. This scorching could have been caused by the 1897 fire, which would indicate the building was there when that fire roared. If the maps are accurate, it may date to before the Civil War and the time of William H. Fowle.

The corporation reports it is making efforts to have oceangoing freighters use the Point Lumley facilities again. Even now, Coast Guard vessels and an occasional tall ship tie up to the corporation's dock. Then, old Point Lumley briefly appears somewhat like it did when Hooe and Harrison loaded flour, wheat and tobacco on ships bound for Baltimore, Martinique and Cádiz.

TODAY (2023)

Except for the old office building, the other buildings of the Robinson Terminal Warehouse Corporation are gone. In their place is a "mixed-use residential community featuring 26 elevator townhomes and 70 luxury condominiums" called Robinson Landing.

Part of old sailing ship discovered partially under wall supporting Wolfe Street. *Alexandria Archaeology.*

As the new landing was being built, however, parts of the port of Alexandria's history emerged. Archaeologists found, in the ground underneath where the corporation's buildings once stood, the foundations of Hooe and Harrison's warehouse and large sections of three old wooden sailing ships of the type that once sailed to and from Alexandria. The warehouse foundations were reburied, but the three ships have been removed and submerged in an Alexandrian pond to preserve them for future study and display. A tangible part of the Duke-to-Wolfe block's history survives.

Chapter 11

SITTING PRETTY COMFORTABLY

Reflections on a Relaxing Pastime, September 1996

O n a clear, mild weekend when everyone wants to be outdoors—riding a bike, playing tennis, working in the yard, hiking—some of us tend to sit.

It is a quiet pastime, but it requires preparation—and thought—to do well. It is, in fact, essential to pick a good spot, be well-provisioned and use your imagination.

On a brisk Saturday morning not long ago, I pulled into a parking space near my objective, the municipal boat dock in Alexandria, on the Potomac near the foot of King Street. Before proceeding to the dock, I stopped at Fire Hook Bakery on North Lee Street and picked up a large cup of coffee and a piece of cinnamon streusel poundcake. Then I walked the half block to King Street, down the shop-lined sidewalk, through the arcade at the Torpedo Factory and onto the dock. I eased onto a bench near its end, careful not to spill my coffee.

To my left, I could see the Capitol dome in the distance across a calming expanse of barely rippling water. Docked in front of me was the *Cherry Blossom*, a white, three-decked riverboat with a paddle wheel at the stern and an iron railing encircling each deck. On my right nearby was the black-hulled, three-masted tall ship *Alexandria*.

Few tourists were about yet. The rain that started the night before had just stopped, and it had kept them inside—prime sitting conditions.

I took a bite of moist, crumbly poundcake and a sip of coffee and shifted slightly on the bench to make my seat more comfortable. The sun was just

Dock at Alexandria waterfront. *Author's collection.*

beginning to send light through the overcast sky. A mallard was quacking from somewhere to my left.

Out on the river, the only thing moving was a single sailboat motoring slowly toward the dock. Its large sail had been lowered and tied to the boom in two lumps, and its small sail lay collapsed in a heap on its foredeck. At the wheel stood a man in bright yellow oilskin pants. An attractive young woman in a thick sweater stood on the foredeck coiling a rope.

I began to wonder idly if they had spent a cold night anchored somewhere on the lower Potomac, and I shivered slightly. Instead, maybe they were from a plantation downriver and had sailed out early this morning in the rain on an urgent errand, or perhaps this was only their usual, elegant morning trip to get coffee and the paper.

Unfortunately, they motored on by and docked at another pier, so I could not inquire. On the other hand, I did not have to move from my seat to ask, either.

I noticed some movement on the *Cherry Blossom* and looked up to see against the sky five or six young men in black suits, white shirts and bow ties walking silently in single file out of the small captain's cabin at the very top of the boat. Leading them was a woman wearing dark glasses. Her legs, clad in tight, black leotards, moved gracefully below a fiery red cloak. She looked back to make sure they were following.

Down the white steps to the next deck they came, down more steps to the even lower deck, and then they disappeared into the heart of the boat. Were they new riverboat men being led to the site of a sensuous initiation rite? Or were they waiters being given a tour of the boat before helping with a party?

Nothing was happening on the *Alexandria*, so I looked farther down on my right to the Robinson Terminal. From time to time, late at night, oceangoing freighters from Scandinavia or eastern Europe sailed in through the Woodrow Wilson drawbridge and docked there to unload.

Earlier, I had noticed signs on several large warehouses near the terminal reading, "SMALL ARMS AMMUNITION" and "WARNING: ENTRY STRICTLY FORBIDDEN." Another sign said the warehouses belonged to "INTERARMS—Importers, Exporters, Manufacturers—Manchester, England; Monte Carlo, Monaco." At the bottom of that sign were the names of German, Spanish and Brazilian small-arms makers.

I pictured a cool night and a forklift towing a snaking line of carts across the dock, each carrying a pallet stacked high with long wooden rifle cases. It stops at the side of the freighter. From high aboard, a crane hovers until camouflage-clad workers attach its lines to the first pallet, and it creaks as it lifts the load onboard under the low-voiced orders of a Dutch-speaking sea captain with a missing foot.

Somehow, though, this seemed like cheating—no ship actually was docked at the terminal.

I shifted focus to the *Alexandria* and imagined stepping on deck, ordering my hand-picked crew to hoist sails and making off for the almond groves and beaches of Majorca as the drawbridge operator opened up during rush hour, backing up traffic along I-95 to Fredericksburg and Annapolis.

I had finished my coffee and cake, and the sun had come out completely from behind the clouds. It was now almost noon. People were milling around. Some were guests for what was clearly a catered wedding on the

Cherry Blossom. Others were filling the tour boats behind me, the *Admiral Tilp* and the *Matthew Hayes*. It was time to leave.

If you were on the dock that Saturday, you likely would have noticed, and imagined, entirely different things. Perhaps you would have chosen a different spot to sit—the fountain at Dupont Circle, the Dumbarton Oaks gardens, the Farm Women's Cooperative Market in Bethesda or somewhere else. Maybe you prefer doughnuts to poundcake for provisions. Whatever you like, of course. The important thing is to sit and let your thoughts be active.

As for me, I ended the morning by walking slowly back across the dock to King Street and stopping in at the Fish Market for a lunch of shrimp and beer over a few pages from a book of gale-force sea stories.

NOTE: IN CASE YOU were wondering, as you well may be, the author did *not* use his imagination in the first ten chapters. Those actually are all factual.

SELECTED BIBLIOGRAPHY

Only the principal sources are listed.

Chapter 1

Fausz, J. Frederick. "Middlemen in Peace and War: Virginia's Earliest Indian Interpreters, 1608–1632." *Virginia Magazine of History and Biography* 95 (January 1987): 41–64.

Haile, Edward Wright, ed. *Jamestown Narratives: Eyewitness Accounts of the Virginia Colony, The First Decades: 1607–1617*. Champlain, VA: RoundHouse, 1998.

Horn, James, ed. *Captain John Smith: Writings with Other Narratives of Roanoke, Jamestown, and the First English Settlement of America*. New York: Library of America, 2007.

Neill, Edward D. *The Founders of Maryland as Portrayed in Manuscripts, Provincial Records and Early Documents*. Albany: Joel Munsell, 1876.

Potter, Stephen R. *Commoners, Tribute, and Chiefs: The Development of Algonquian Culture in the Potomac Valley*. Charlottesville: University of Virginia Press, 1993.

Rice, James D. *Nature and History in the Potomac Country: From Hunter-Gatherers to the Age of Jefferson*. Baltimore: Johns Hopkins University Press, 2009.

Roundtree, Helen C. *The Powhatan Indians of Virginia: Their Traditional Culture*. Norman: University of Oklahoma Press, 1989.

Chapter 2

Brugger, Robert J. *Maryland: A Middle Temperament 1634–1980*. Baltimore: Johns Hopkins University Press, 1988.

Carr, Lois Green. "Margaret Brent—A Brief History." Maryland State Archives Online, 2002. https://msa.maryland.gov/msa/speccol/sc3500/sc3520/002100/002177/html/mbrent2.html.

Library of Virginia. Virginia Land Patents and Grants, September 6, 1654, Patent Book 3, p. 275. Accessed August 3, 2022. https://lva-virginia.libguides.com/land-grants.

Maryland State Archives. Archives of Maryland Online. Various entries, principally vol. 10, p. 4; vol. 41, p. 460; vol. 4, p. 367. https://msa.maryland.gov.

Moxham, Robert Morgan. *The Great Hunting Creek Land Grants*. North Springfield, VA: Colonial Press, 1974.

Robinson, W. Stitt, Jr. *Mother Earth: Land Grants in Virginia, 1607–1699*. Charlottesville: University Press of Virginia, 1957.

Somerville, Mollie. "Lady of the Manor." In *A Composite History of Alexandria*, Elizabeth Hambleton and Marian Van Landingham, eds. Alexandria: Alexandria Bicentennial Commission (1975), 1–5.

Chapter 3

Abbot, W.W., ed. *The Papers of George Washington, Colonial Series*. Vol. 1, *1748–August 1755*. Charlottesville: University Press of Virginia, 1983.

Bailey, Kenneth P. *The Ohio Company of Virginia and the Westward Movement, 1748–1792*. 1939; reprint, Lewisburg, PA: Wennawoods Publishing, 2000.

Brock, R.A., ed. *The Official Records of Robert Dinwiddie, Lieutenant-Governor of the Colony of Virginia, 1751–1758*. Vol. 1. Richmond: Virginia Historical Society, 1833.

Brown, Stuart E. *Virginia Baron: The Story of Thomas 6th Lord Fairfax*. Baltimore: Chesapeake Book Company, 1965.

Calloway, Colin G. *The Indian World of George Washington: The First President, the First Americans, and the Birth of the Nation*. New York: Oxford University Press, 2018.

Darlington, William M. *Christopher Gist's Journals with Historical, Geographical and Ethnological Notes and Biographies of His Contemporaries*. 1893; reprint with new material, Westminster, MD: Heritage Books, 2002.

Goodman, Alfred T., ed. *Journal of Captain William Trent from Logstown to Pickawillany, A.D. 1752*. Cincinnati: Robert Clarke, 1871.

Hanna, Charles A. *The Wilderness Trail*. Vol. 1. New York: G.P. Putnam's Sons, 1911.

Hinderaker, Eric. *Elusive Empires: Constructing Colonialism in the Ohio Valley, 1763–1800*. Cambridge: Cambridge University Press, 1997.

Hofstra, Warren R. *The Planting of New Virginia: Settlement and Landscape in the Shenandoah Valley*. Baltimore: Johns Hopkins University Press, 2004.

Hunter, William A. *Forts on the Pennsylvania Frontier, 1753–1758*. Harrisburg: Commonwealth of Pennsylvania, Pennsylvania Historical and Museum Commission, 1960.

Jennings, Francis. *Empire of Fortune: Crowns, Colonies & Tribes in the Seven Years War in America*. New York: W.W. Norton, 1988.

Kent, Donald H. *The French Invasion of Western Pennsylvania, 1753*. Harrisburg: Commonwealth of Pennsylvania, Pennsylvania Historical and Museum Commission, 1954.

Merrell, James H. "'The Cast of His Countenance': Reading Andrew Montour," in Ronald Hoffman, Mechal Sobel and Fredrika J. Teute, eds. *Through a Glass Darkly: Reflections on Personal Identity in Early America*. Williamsburg: Omohundro Institute of Early American History & Culture (1997), 13-39.

———. *Into the American Woods: Negotiations on the Pennsylvania Frontier*. New York: W.W. Norton, 2000.

"Minutes of the Winchester Conference," contained in a report from William Fairfax to the Honorable Robert Dinwiddie, Lieutenant Governor of Virginia. Library of Congress, Manuscript Reading Room, British Public Record Office, Records of the British Colonial Office, Class 5, file 1328, pages 43–72. These minutes are the major source for this chapter.

Mulkearn, Lois, ed. *George Mercer Papers Relating to the Ohio Company of Virginia*. Pittsburgh: University of Pittsburg Press, 1954.

Parkman, Francis. *France and England in North American*. Vol. 2. New York: Library of America, 1983.

Sheehan, Bernard W. *Savagism and Civility: Indians and Englishmen in Colonial Virginia*. Cambridge: Cambridge University Press, 1980.

Sipe, C. Hale. *The Indian Chiefs of Pennsylvania*. Lewisburg, PA: Wennawoods Publishing, 1997.

State of Pennsylvania. *Minutes of the Provincial Council of Pennsylvania from the Organization to the Termination of the Proprietary Government*. Vol. 5. Harrisburg: Theo. Fenn, 1851.

Volwiler, Albert T. *George Croghan and the Westward Movement, 1741–1782.* Cleveland: Arthur H. Clark Company, 1926.

Wallace, Paul A.W. *Indians in Pennsylvania.* 2nd ed. Harrisburg: Pennsylvania Historical and Museum Commission, 1993.

White, Richard. *The Middle Ground: Indians, Empires, and Republics in the Great Lakes Region, 1650–1815.* New York: Cambridge University Press, 1991.

Chapter 4

Abbott, W.W., ed. *The Papers of George Washington.* Colonial Series 1, 1748– August 1755. Charlottesville: University of Virginia Press, 1983.

Anderson, Fred. *Crucible of War: The Seven Years' War and the Fate of Empire in British North America, 1754–1766.* New York: Alfred A. Knopf, 2000.

Braddock, Edward. Letter to the Honorable Thomas Robinson, April 19, 1755, and other letters in Moreau, Jacob Nicolas. *A Memorial, Containing a Summary View of Facts with Their Authorities, in Answer to the Observations Sent by the English Ministry to the Courts of Europe.* Philadelphia: James Chattin, 1757.

"Braddock's Campaign and the Potomac Route to the West." Pamphlet printed by Higher Education Publications, Falls Church, Virginia (1997). Reprint from the *Winchester-Frederick County Historical Society Journal* 1 (1986).

Brands, H.W. *The First American: The Life and Times of Benjamin Franklin.* New York, Doubleday, 2000.

Hamilton, Charles, ed. *Braddock's Defeat: The Journal of Captain Robert Cholmley's Batman, the Journal of a British Officer, Colonel Sir Peter Halkett's Orderly Book.* Norman: University of Oklahoma Press, 1959.

Kammen, Michael. *Colonial New York: A History.* New York: Charles Scribner's Sons, 1975.

Kopperman, Paul E. *Braddock at the Monongahela.* Pittsburgh: University of Pittsburgh Press, 1977.

MacLeod, Malcolm. "Lienard De Beaujeu, Daniel-Hyacinthe-Marie." In the Dictionary of Canadian Biography Online, accessed October 25, 2005, and July 8, 2022. www.biographi.ca/en/bio/lienard_de_beaujeu_ daniel_hyacinthe_marie_3E.html.

McCardell, Lee. *Ill-Starred General: Braddock of the Coldstream Guards.* Pittsburgh: University of Pittsburgh Press, 1958.

Munson, James D. *Colo. John Carlyle, Gent.: A True and Just Account of the Man and His House 1720–1780.* Fairfax Station: Northern Virginia Regional Park Authority, 1986.

Netherton, Ross D. "The Carlyle House Conference: An Episode in the Politics of Colonial Union." Paper prepared for a Conference of Northern Virginia Studies on "Alexandria: Empire to Commonwealth," Alexandria, Virginia, October 14–15, 1983. Files, Carlyle House.

Nichols, Franklin Thayer. "The Organization of Braddock's Army." *William and Mary Quarterly*, third series, vol. 4 (1947), 125–47.

Pargellis, Stanley, ed. *Military Affairs in North America 1748–1765: Selected Documents from the Cumberland Papers in Windsor Castle*. Reprint of the 1936 edition, Hamden, CT: Archon Books, 1969.

Wahll, Andrew J. *Braddock Road Chronicles 1755 from Diaries and Records of Members of the Braddock Expedition and Others*. Bowie, MD: Heritage Books, 1999.

Chapter 5

Alexandria Gazette. (During the war, the *Gazette* was known by different names, but in this book, it is called simply the *Alexandria Gazette*.)

American State Papers: Documents Legislative and Executive of the Congress of the United States. Class 5, Military Affairs, vol. 1. Washington: Gates and Seaton, 1832. https://memory.loc.gov/ammem/amlaw/lwsp.html.

Artisans and Merchants of Alexandria, 1780–1820. Vols. 1 and 2. Bowie, MD: Heritage Books, 2008, 2019.

Borneman, Walter R. *1812: The War That Forged a Nation*. New York: Harper, 2005.

Brown, Thomas. "An Account of the Lineage of the Browne Family." Vol. 2. Ambler-Brown Family Papers, 1780–1865. Rubenstein Library, Manuscripts, Library Service Center, Box 1, c. 1. Duke University, Durham, NC.

Butler, Stuart L. *Defending the Old Dominion: Virginia and Its Militia in the War of 1812*. Lanham, MD: University Press of America, 2013.

"Claims for Slaves Captured by the British in the War of 1812." National Archives and Records Administration, College Park, Maryland. Copies in the Alexandria Archaeology Museum, Alexandria, Virginia.

Crawford, Michael J., ed. *The Naval War of 1812: A Documentary History*. Vol. 3, 1814–1815. Washington, D.C.: Naval Historical Center, 2002.

Daily National Intelligencer (Washington, D.C.).

Dudley, William S., ed. *The Naval War of 1812: A Documentary History*. Vols. 1 (1812) and 2 (1813) Washington, D.C.: Naval Historical Center, 1985, 1992.

Eshelman, Ralph E., and Burton K. Kummerow. *In Full Glory Reflected: Discovering the War of 1812 in the Chesapeake.* Crownsville: Maryland Historical Trust, 2012.

Hickey, Donald R. *The War of 1812: A Forgotten Conflict.* Champaign: University of Illinois Press, 2012.

Hollan, Catherine B. *Virginia Silversmiths, Jewelers, Clock and Watch-Makers, 1607–1860, Their Lives and Marks.* MacLean, VA: Hollan Press, 2010.

Miller, T. Michael. *Pen Portraits of Alexandria, Virginia, 1739–1900.* Bowie, MD: Heritage Books, 1987.

Morgan, James Dudley. "Historic Fort Washington on the Potomac." *Records of the Columbia Historical Society* 7 (1895), 1–19

Munson, Jim. "Sights and Sounds of Alexandria in 1800." Volunteer training materials, Gadsby's Tavern Museum, Alexandria, Virginia.

Napier, Elers. *The Life and Correspondence of Admiral Sir Charles Napier, K.C.B. from Personal Recollections, Letters, and Official Documents.* Vol. 1. Reprint: Chestnut Hill, MA: Elibron Classics/Adamant Media Corporation, 2005. Original publisher: London: Hurst & Blackett, 1862.

National Archives. Military Records, War of 1812. Through Fold3.com.

Norton, Richard Cranch. Papers. Massachusetts Historical Society.

Nunn, Joan. *Fashion in Costume: 1200–2000.* Chicago: New Amsterdam Books, 1998.

O'Neill, Patrick L. *To Annoy or Destroy the Enemy: The Battle of the White House After the Burning of Washington.* Privately published, 2014.

Pitch, Anthony. *The Burning of Washington: The British Invasion of 1814.* Annapolis: Naval Institute Press, 1998.

Pool, Daniel. *What Jane Austen Ate and Charles Dickens Knew: From Fox Hunting to Whist—the Facts of Everyday Life in 19th-Century England.* New York: Touchstone, 1994.

Pope, Michael Lee. *The Hidden History of Alexandria, D.C.* Charleston, SC: The History Press, 2011.

Porter, David Dixon. *Memoir of Commodore David Porter, of the United States Navy.* Albany: J. Munsell, Publisher, 1875.

Richmond Enquirer.

Sims, Charles. Papers. Library of Congress.

Taylor, Alan. *The Internal Enemy: Slavery and War in Virginia, 1772–1732.* New York: W.W. Norton, 2013.

Toll, Ian W. *Six Frigates: The Epic History of the Founding of the U.S. Navy.* New York: W.W. Norton, 2006.

Vogel, Steve. *Through the Perilous Fight: Six Weeks That Saved the Nation.* New York: Random House, 2013.

Williams, John S. *History of the Invasion and Capture of Washington and the Events That Preceded and Followed.* New York: Harper & Brothers, 1857.

Will of John Wise. Alexandria Orphans Court. *Will Book 2.*

Chapter 6

Green, Constance McLaughlin. *Washington: Village and Capital, 1800–1878.* Princeton, NJ: Princeton University Press, 1962.

Morley, Jefferson. *Snow-Storm in August: Washington City Francis Scott Key, and the Forgotten Race Riot of 1835.* New York: Doubleday, 2012.

National Park Service, Department of the Interior. Historic Building Survey, Judiciary Square, circa 1933.

Record Group 21, Records of District Courts of the United States, National Archive Microfilm Publications, Microcopy No. 434, Habeas Corpus Case Records of the United States Circuit Court for the District of Columbia, 1820–1863, Roll 1, 1820–1843, images 0455, 0459–0465.

Sheahan, James W. *Corporation Laws of the City of Washington, to the End of the Fiftieth Council.* Washington, D.C.: Robert A. Waters, 1853.

Snethen, Worthington G. *The Black Code of the District of Columbia, in Force September 1st, 1848.* New York: William Harned, 1848.

Chapter 7

Comings, H.H. *Personal Reminiscence of Co. E, N.Y. Fire Zouaves Better Known as Ellsworth's Fire Zouaves.* Malden, MA: J. Gould Tilden, Steam Book and Job Printers, 1886.

Doon, Ellen. *Guide to the M.D. Ball Papers.* New Haven: Yale University Library, 2000.

Dowdey, Clifford, and Louis H. Manarin, eds. *The Wartime Papers of R.E. Lee.* New York: Bramhall House, 1961.

Glasgow, William M., Jr. *Northern Virginia's Own: The 17th Virginia Infantry Regiment, Confederate States of America.* Alexandria: Gobill Press, 1989.

House, Edward H. "The Taking of Alexandria: Full Details of the Movement, Tearing Down the Rebel Flag, the Murder of Col. Ellsworth, Minute and Accurate Account." *New York Tribune*, May 26, 1961.

Netherton, Nan, et al. *Fairfax County, Virginia: A History.* Fairfax: Fairfax County Board of Supervisors, 1978.

Pohanka, Brian C., and Patrick A. Schroeder, eds. *With the 11th New York Fire Zouaves in Camp, Battle, and Prison: The Narrative of Private Arthur O'Neil Alcock in the New York Atlas and Leader*. Lynchburg: Schroeder, 2011.

Scott, Robert Garth, ed. *Forgotten Valor: The Memoirs, Journals & Civil War Letters of Orlando B. Willcox*. Kent, OH: Kent State University Press, 1999.

Time-Life Books, eds. *Voices of the Civil War: First Manassas*. Alexandria: Time-Life, 1997.

United States Navy War Records Office. *Official Records of the Union and Confederate Navies in the War of the Rebellion*, 1:4. Washington: U.S. Government Printing Office, 1894–1922.

United States War Department. *War of Rebellion: A Compilation of the Official Records of the Union and Confederate Armies*, 1:2. Washington: U.S. Government Printing Office, 1880–1901.

Warfield, Edgar. *Manassas to Appomattox: The Civil War Memoirs of Pvt. Edgar Warfield, 17th Virginia Infantry*. McLean, VA: EPM Publications, 1996.

Zimmerman, John R. *Diary of John R. Zimmerman*. Unpublished, Box 113, Manuscripts Section, Local History/Special Collections Branch, Alexandria Public Library.

Chapter 8

Alexandria Gazette. August 8, 1904; January 2, 6, 7, 9, 10, 11, 14, 19, 1905; May 4, 6, 8, 1929; December 18, 1945.

Crabill, Robert L. "Town of Potomac." *Alexandria History* 4 (1982).

Escherich, Susan. "The Development of Suburban Alexandria: Del Ray and St. Elmo." *Fireside Sentinel*, May 1992.

———. "The Town of Potomac." *Fireside Sentinel*, August 1992.

Fischman, Robert, and Antoinette Fischman. Interview with an archaeology volunteer. November 1, 2005. Alexandria Archaeology Museum.

Fleishman, Sandra. "Alexandria's Del Ray, a Neighborhood Rediscovered." *Washington Post*, March 16, 2002.

Gaillot, Ed, and Shirley Gaillot. Interview with an archaeology volunteer. November 13, 2004. Archaeology Museum.

Grimm, Norman. Interview with an archaeology volunteer. April 1, 2005. Alexandria Archaeology Museum.

Grimm, Ralph. Interview with an archaeology volunteer. November 23, 2005. Alexandria Archaeology Museum.

Hatch, Norm. Interview with Dave Mills, archaeology volunteer. March 20, 2008. Alexandria Archaeology Museum.

McArtor, Maria Patricia Downey. Interview with Barbara Murray, archaeology volunteer. July 22, 2008. Alexandria Archaeology Museum.

Mills, Vernon. "The Forgotten Town: The Saga of Short-Lived Potomac, Va." *Alexandria Gazette Packet*, August 24, 1917.

National Register of Historic Places Registration Form. National Park Service, United States Department of Interior. DHR File No. 100–136, "Town of Potomac." August 9, 1991.

Partlow, Nora. Interview in *Zebra*, March 2019.

Perna, Lee. "Del Ray's First House." *Del Ray Citizen*, December 2008.

Pulliam, Ted. *Historic Alexandria: An Illustrated History*. San Antonio: Historical Publishing Network, 2011.

Schulte, Brigid. "This Year, Marking a Scrappy Start: Centennial Celebrations Will Revisit Del Ray's Juicy History of Gambling, Protests and Enterprise." *Washington Post*, March 6, 2008.

Town of Potomac Historical Association. "The History of the Del Ray Neighborhoods." https://www.potomacva.org.

Warthen, Shirley Grimm. Interview with an archaeology volunteer. October 18, 2003. Alexandria Archaeology Museum.

Washington Post. March 16, 30, October 14, 16, 1894; January 10, 12, 15, 19, 1905.

Wood, Bob. "Del Ray and the Death of the Ducky Boys." Del Ray Citizens Association News, March 17, 2013.

Chapter 9

Blumenson, Martin. *The Patton Papers, 1885–1940*. Vols. 1 and 2. Boston: Houghton Mifflin Company, 1972.

Cavalry School. *Employment of Cavalry, 1924–1925*. Fort Riley, KS: Cavalry School, Department of General Instruction, 1924.

Chandler, William E. "26th Cavalry (PS)—Battles to Glory." *Armored Cavalry Journal* 56, no. 2 (March–April 1947), 11–16; no. 3 (May–June 1947), 7–15; no. 4 (July–August 1947), 15–22.

Daley, John Leslie Sanderson. "From Theory to Practice: Tanks, Doctrine, and the U.S. Army, 1916–1940." Doctoral dissertation DA9403192, Kent State University, 1993.

Dayhuff, Charles H., Jr. "First Classmen Report on R.O.T.C. Camps: Fort Myer." *Cadet* 24 (September 15, 1930).

———. Interview with author, February 27, 1988, Paoli, Pennsylvania.

D'Este, Carlo. *Patton: A Genius for War*. New York: HarperCollins, 1995.

Gillie, Mildred Hanson. *Forging the Thunderbolt*. Harrisburg, PA: Military Service Publishing, 1947.

Harmon, Ernest N. "The Second Cavalry in the St. Mihiel Offensive." *Cavalry Journal* 30, no. 124 (July 1921), 10–18.

Herr, John K. "Cavalry Affairs Before Congress." *Cavalry Journal* 48, no. 212 (March–April 1939), 130–135.

Johnson, David E. *Fast Tanks and Heavy Bombers: Innovation in the U.S. Army, 1917–1945*. Ithaca: Cornell University Press, 1998.

Leavel, Byrd S., ed. "Ft. Myer." *Bomb* (1931), 210.

Patton, George S., Jr., and C.C. Benson. "Mechanization and Cavalry." *Cavalry Journal* 39, no. 159 (April 1930): 234–240.

———. "Motorization and Mechanization in the Cavalry," *Cavalry Journal* 39, no. 160 (July 1930): 331–348.

———. "Mechanized Forces." *Cavalry Journal* 42, no. 179 (September–October 1933): 5–8.

Ramsey, Edwin Price, and Stephen J. Rivele. *Lieutenant Ramsey's War: From Horse Soldier to Guerrilla Commander*. Washington, D.C.: Brassey's, 1990.

Stanton, Doug. *Horse Soldiers: The Extraordinary Story of a Band of U.S. Soldiers Who Rode to Victory in Afghanistan*. New York: Scribner, 2009.

Stubbs, Mary Lee, and Stanley Russell Connor. *Armor-Cavalry Part I*. Washington, D.C.: Government Printing Office, 1969.

Truscott, Lucian K., Jr. *The Twilight of the U.S. Cavalry: Life in the Old Army, 1917–1942*. Lawrence: University Press of Kansas, 1989.

Unknown Polish officer in translation. "Training of Modern Cavalry for War: Polish Cavalry Doctrine." *Cavalry Journal* 48, no. 214 (July–August 1939): 298–306, 315.

Wheeler, Captain John. "Action Report 26th Cavalry—January 16, 1943." *Life* 12, no. 9 (March 2, 1942): 51–55.

Wheeler-Nicholson, Malcolm. *Modern Cavalry*. New York: Macmillan, 1922.

Wills, Charles L. Interview with the author, May 14, 1988, Weldon, North Carolina.

Chapter 10

Books and Articles

Abbott, W.W., and Dorothy Twohig, eds. *The Papers of George Washington, Presidential Series.* Vol. 2, *April –June 1789.* Charlottesville: University Press of Virginia, 1987.

Bookin-Weiner, Jerome B., and Mohamed El Mansour, eds. *The Atlantic Connection: Moroccan-American Relations, 1786–1986.* Edino Press, 1990.

Clark, William Bell, ed. *Naval Documents of the American Revolution.* Vols. 3 and 4. Washington, D.C.: U.S. Government Printing Office, 1968.

Du Pont, B.G., trans. *Life of Eleuthere Irenee DuPont from Contemporary Correspondence, 1819–1934.* Vol. 11. Newark: University of Delaware Press, 1926.

Jackson, Donald, and Dorothy Twohig, eds. *The Diaries of George Washington.* Vols. 2, 3 and 4. Charlottesville: University Press of Virginia, 1976, 1978.

Kundahl, George G. *Alexandria Goes to War.* Knoxville: University of Tennessee Press, 2004.

Miller, T. Michael, ed. *A Partial Transcript of the Correspondence of the Business Firm of Hooe and Harrison.* Local History/Special Collections, Alexandria Library.

———. *Artisans and Merchants of Alexandria, Virginia, 1780–1820.* Vol. 1. Bowie, MD: Heritage Books, 1991.

———. *Pen Portraits of Alexandria, Virginia.* Bowie, MD: Heritage Books, 1987.

Morgan, William James, ed. *Naval Documents of the American Revolution.* Vol. 5. Washington, D.C.: U.S. Government Printing Office, 1970.

Pippenger, Wesley E. *Alexandria, Virginia Life in 1850: The Diary of Ella Hooe Fowle, 1832–1855.* Arlington: Wesley E. Pippenger, 1999.

"Proceedings of the Trustees of the Town of Alexandria, Virginia, 1749–1778, 1793–1800," Northern Virginia Conservation Council Exhibit in the Case *United States v. Bryant.* Unpublished (VA REF, Local History/Special Collections Branch, Alexandria Library).

Pulliam, Ted. "Point Lumley, Its Location, Appearance, and Structures." Unpublished paper, 2006. Alexandria Archaeology Museum.

Shephard, Steven J. "Reaching for the Channel." *Alexandria Chronicle* (Spring 2006).

Shomette, Donald G. *Maritime Alexandria.* Bowie, MD: Heritage Books, 2003.

Sparacio, Ruth, and Sam Sparacio, eds. *Abstracts of Land Clauses, Prince William County, Virginia, 1789–1790.* Bowie, MD: Antient Press, 1972.

Speare, Elizabeth George. *Life in Colonial America*. New York: Random House, 1963.

Sprouse, Edith Moore, transcriber. *Harry Piper Letter Book 1767–1775*. Alexandria: n.p., 1991.

Stephenson, Richard W., ed. *The Cartography of Northern Virginia*. Fairfax: Fairfax County, 1981.

Unlisted author. "Robinson on the Waterfront." *Alexandrian Magazine* 3, no. 2 (1977).

Williams, Ames W. "Transportation." In *Alexandria: A Towne in Transition, 1800–1900*, Macoll and Stansfield, eds. Alexandria: Alexandria Bicentennial Commission, 1977.

Other Sources

Adams, John. Letter to John Jay, Secretary of State (London, February 25, 1787). National Archives, Record Group 360, Papers of the Continental Congress, M247, R113, item 84, vol. 6, fol. 427.

Circular. "TO THE PUBLIC." January 22, 1828, a reprint by Lewis A. Cazenove of a circular published by William Fowle (copy located in the Cazenove folder in the "vertical files" in the Local History/Special Collections, Barrett Library, Alexandria, Virginia).

Interview with Robert W. "Willie" Taylor, operations manager, Robinson Terminal Warehouse Corporation, July 6, 2006 (Duke-Wolfe Street research files, Alexandria Archaeology Museum, Alexandria, Virginia).

Map. "Wharfs Storehouses Etc." A Civil War–era map showing buildings between Prince and Wolfe Streets on the waterfront, drafter not listed (located in Map Drawer 4, Local History/Special Collections, Barrett Library, Alexandria, Virginia).

Will of Robert Townshend Hooe, Alexandria Will Book C.

ABOUT THE AUTHOR

 Ted Pulliam's articles, some of which are included in this book, have appeared in *Legal Times*, *WWII History* magazine, *American History* magazine, the *Washington Post* and other publications. He is author of *Historic Alexandria: An Illustrated History*, published by the City of Alexandria. A current member of the Alexandria Archaeological Commission and the Alexandria African Heritage Trail Committee, he also is a past member of the board of the Alexandria Historical Society and the Alexandria Waterfront Commission. He received the award given annually by the historical society for making "especially noteworthy contributions to the preservation of the historic, cultural and artistic heritage of Alexandria." He is a graduate of Davidson College and Columbia University Law School and lives in the Del Ray part of Alexandria.